BITTER SWEET

BITTER SWEET

Indigenous Women in the Pacific

Edited by

ALISON JONES, PHYLLIS HERDA
& TAMASAILAU M. SUAALII

University of Otago Press

Published by University of Otago Press
56 Union Street/PO Box 56, Dunedin, New Zealand
Fax: 64 3 479 8385
email: university.press@stonebow.otago.ac.nz

First published 2000

ISBN 1 877133 87 6

Cover image: *Lālange*, by Dagmar Vaikalafi Dyck

Printed by PrintLink Ltd, Wellington

Contents

Notes on Contributors

Jacqui Sutton Beets lives in Lower Hutt and has recently completed an MA in English Literature at Massey University. Her publications include children's stories, three young adult novels and some poetry. In her spare time she enjoys writing music.

Helene Connor is of Maori and Irish descent. Her iwi is Te Atiawa and her hapū is Ngati Rahiri. She is completing her PhD which investigates the genre of biography, both as a branch of literature and history and as a research methodology. She is also writing the biography of a prominent Māori woman community worker. She tutors and lectures part-time in Women's Studies at the University of Auckland.

Phyllis Herda's research and teaching interests include gender, power and colonisation, oral tradition as history and the production and presentation of textiles in the Pacific. Her academic background is in Anthropology and Pacific History. Currently, she is working on a project on women's quilting in Polynesia and is a Senior Lecturer in Women's Studies at the University of Auckland. Phyllis was editor of the *Woman's Studies Journal* between 1996 and 1999.

Te Kawehau Clea Hoskins. Tenā koutou katoa. He mihi nui ēnei ki a koutou katoa e whai kaha tonu nei ke te whawhai, ki te kawe, i a rā, i a rā, ngā kaupapa maha hei whakaora ai te iwi. Mā a koutou mahi tātou ka hapai, ka tū pakari ai. Heoi, e tika ana te whakatauākī 'ehara tāku toa i te toa takitahi, engari ko te toa takitini'. Nō reira tātou mā kua takoto te mānuka, kawea ake! Te Kawehau is currently completing a Masters degree and tutoring in Māori Education at the University of Auckland.

Alison Jones is a Senior Lecturer in Education, and Director of the Institute for Research on Gender, at the University of Auckland. She has published widely on gender and ethnicity in education, including the ethnography *'At School I've got a Chance' Culture/Privilege: Pacific Islands and Pakeha Girls at School* (Dunmore Press, 1991). She was also on the editorial board of the *Women's Studies Journal* from 1996 to 1999.

Jacqueline Leckie is a Senior Lecturer in Social Anthropology at the University of Otago and previously taught at the University of the South Pacific and Kenyatta University, Nairobi. Her publications focus on labour, gender, migration, and ethnicity in the South Pacific and South Asia. A recent publication with University of Otago Press was *To Labour with the State*. She is also a co-author of *Labour in the South Pacific* and has begun to write a history of 'institutionalised madness' in Fiji.

Selina Tusitala Marsh is of Samoan, Tuvalu and English descent. She is currently working on a doctorate at the University of Auckland, examining the tensions of race and gender in the poetry of Pacific Islands women. She has recently returned from Hawai'i on a combined Fulbright scholarship and East-West Centre fellowship. She is also a practising poet.

Tamasailau M. Suaalii is currently undertaking full-time doctoral studies in Sociology at the University of Auckland. She also holds a part-time Assistant Research Fellow position with the Pacific Health Research Centre, Department of Maori and Pacific Health, University of Auckland. She has a wide socio-legal interest in ethnic minority issues, particularly in relation to Sāmoan communities.

Lonise Tanielu is a Samoan educator who has worked with Pasifika communities and students for over twenty years. In the last three years she has held a part-time lectureship in the School of Education at Auckland University which involved her in the teaching and administration of education courses with Pacific content, and monitoring of Pasifika students. She is currently completing PhD research on Sāmoan pastor schools.

Konai Helu Thaman is Tongan and is currently Professor of Pacific Education and Culture, and Head of the School of Humanities at the University of the South Pacific. She also holds a UNESCO Chair in Teacher Education and Culture. She is a widely published poet. Four collections of her poetry have been published by Mana Publications: *You, the Choice of My Parents; Langakali; Hingano* and *Kakala*. One collection, *Inselfuer*, is a German translation of poems from the first two collections.

AnneMarie Tupuola is a New Zealand-born Samoan, and she is a PhD student in Education at Victoria University. She also teaches on such topics as adolescent development and Pacific Islands education. Her current research is on the reappropriation of the terms 'adolescence' and 'New Zealand-born Samoan' and involves an exploration of hybrid identities and diaspora feminism.

Judith van Trigt completed a B.A. in Women's Studies at the University of Auckland in 1996. She now writes for television.

Glossary of Māori Words

aroha – love, compassion

Atua – gods

haka – dance (fierce)

hapū - sub-tribe

hāngi – earth oven

hui – gathering/meeting

iwi – tribal group/people

iwi kawa (*kawa o te iwi*) – tribal protocols and customs

karakia – incantation / prayer

karanga – call of welcome and ritual (performed by Māori women)

kaumātua – female or male elders

kaupapa – philosophy, values and principles

kaupapa Māori – Māori philosophies, values, principles and approaches

kauwhau – talk, lecture

kawa – protocols, customs, practices

kohanga reo – total immersion Māori language nests (0–6 yrs)

kōrero – talk

kuia – female elder

kura kaupapa – total immersion Māori language and philosophy schools

mana – spiritual power and authority

Mana Wāhine Māori – the spiritual power and authority of Māori women

manuhiri – visitors, guests

marae – traditional Māori gathering place, the space directly in front of the meeting house

marae kawa (*te kawa o te marae*) – protocols associated with the rituals of encounter.

mauri – life principle/force

mihi – greet, acknowledge

moa – large flightless bird, now extinct

moko – traditional tattoo

mokopuna - grandchild, descendant

Ngāti Porou – tribe from the East Coast region

noa – free from ritual restriction, freedom of action within the limits of tikanga.

Pā – fortified village

paepae tapu – speakers bench

Pākehā – descendants of immigrants from Europe who have been in Aotearoa for several generations

pakiwaitara – legends

Papatuanuku – Earth Mother

patu – hand-held club

poi – ball with short string attached, can be swung rhythmically to the accompaniment of song

pūrakau – ancient oral texts, myths

rangatira – chief/leader, male or female

Ranginui – Sky Father

Rūnanga – tribal councils/trusts

taiaha – a weapon of hard wood

Tainui – ancestral canoe and tribe from the Waikato region

tāngata whenua – people of the land, first peoples/indigenous

taonga – treasure

tapu – set apart under ritual restriction

tauira – pupil under instruction

tauiwi – peoples who are not indigenous

tauparapara – incantation, now often used in speechmaking

Te Arawa – ancestral canoe and tribe from the Rotorua region

te reo Māori – the Māori language
tika – right, correct, straight, direct
tikanga – cultural practices and customs considered to be right and correct
Tino Rangatiratanga – absolute authority, self-determination, sovereignty
tukutuku – patterned wall panels in a meeting house
tūpuna – ancestor living or deceased
tūturu – fixed, permanent, authentic
wāhine – women (pl); *wahine* – woman (s)
waiata – song
wairua – spirit
wānanga – gatherings for learning
wānanga reo – total immersion Māori language learning gatherings
whaikōrero – speechmaking
whakanoa – to make free from ritual restriction
whakapapa – genealogy, descent lines
whakatauaki – proverbial sayings
whānau – extended family group
whare wānanga – Māori philosophy tertiary institutions (traditional houses of learning)
wharehui – meeting house

Glossary of Samoan Words

aoaoina – educated
aoga – school
alofa – love
amio (verb) – to behave, to act
amio (noun) – behaviour, actions
aue – an intermittent response during the telling of a story
faaaloalo – polite, politely
faakerisiano – like a christian
fagogo – legend
faifeau – minister
faitau – read
feagaiga – title of respect given to a church minister which signifies the covenant between him/her and the parish
fesili – question, ask
fetau – a tree with round fruits used as marbles (*calophyllumino-phyllum*)
fune – breadfruit tree buds
itumalo – district
malae – an open outdoor area in the centre of the village for public meetings and entertainments
mapu – marbles
muamua – first or one
paia – holy
palagi/papalagi – European, English
pepe – baby, doll
Pi Tautau – pictorial Samoan alphabet
po – night
poto – clever, smart, intelligent
pulu – name of tree (*capparis*); its budding leaves are rubbed together and blown up as balloons
pulu – coconut husk
sili – first, top of the class, first prize
suega – examination, test
tagigafagogo – chanting of legends
tamaititi – child, student
tauloto – rote-learned bible verse
tautau – hang, hanging
tusi – book
Tusi Paia – holy book, Bible
valea – dumb, stupid, foolish
vasega – class, grade

Introduction

ALISON JONES, PHYLLIS HERDA
& TAMASAILAU M. SUAALII

Indigenous women of the Pacific often speak of the bitter sweetness of this place. Tongan poet Konai Helu Thaman writes in this volume of 'bitter sweet messages' which tell of a potent mix of the bitterness and sweetness of family, colonisation, and the land. Indigenous women in the Pacific constantly negotiate these tensions as they work in, and against, their communities and the institutions in which they labour, and write. Others such as Vanuatu poet Grace Mera Molisa refer to the 'bitter – sweet / fruit / of sovereignty struggle'. For Molisa, the sweet fruit of her country's independence has turned sour because it has proved to be 'for men only'.[1]

The poets' shared metaphor is loaded with the productive energy of opposing forces. In the Pacific, families provide the heart and passion of life, as well as its limitations and sometimes maddening obligations. Colonisation has brought with it many technical benefits, but also the overwhelming bitterness of oppression and poverty. And the sweetness of indigenous gains in struggles for sovereignty and land rights have often been tinged for women with the sour inevitability of male privilege. All of these sites are marked by vigorous talk, analysis, and action. Yet the Pacific has endured centuries of Western framing as a 'sweet' place – a place of oceans and islands, plenitude and beauty. The 'balmy, unchanging, blue Pacific' generated for tourists rarely makes visible the massive effects of the imperialist West, and the attempts of indigenous women and men to re/gain a sense of certainty and sovereignty in the face of an exploitative globalised economic and cultural order.

Despite the satisfyingly apt sense of ambiguity contained in the phrase 'bitter sweet', we chose it as our book title with a certain degree of ambivalence. For Samoan editor Tamasailau Suaalii, the phrase generates discomfort with its inevitably sour after-taste of negativity. According to Suaalii, the experiences of women from the Pacific, when filtered through Western grids of intelligibility, inevitably create and position their /our struggle as contradictory, oppositional and even ambivalent. Paradoxically, she maintains, other ways of thinking have become blurred as we have learned to 'speak' our struggles through Western frames, while we seek at the same time to disrupt them.[2]

Within this always-present paradox (we cannot exist outside colonisation), the authors in this volume 'write down' the complex, bitter sweet politics of women's lives and struggles in the Pacific.

A key feature of the imperialism of Western explorers in the South Pacific since the seventeenth century has been their provisioning of the 'West' with its dreams of exotic beauty and benevolent Nature. The fantasy of the South Pacific has long represented for those of other places the possibilities of a pure space, outside the ambivalences of the 'developed' world. In particular, the manufactured images of the indigenous women of the Pacific embodied these imperial im/possibilities. And ever since the arrival of Western travellers and colonisers, Pacific women have responded by both embracing and critiquing their presence and its effects.

Some of these responses and discussions continue here. Due to a huge demand for published accounts of contemporary research about peoples of the Pacific, this collection of recent work has been reprinted from the *Women's Studies Journal*, the Journal of the New Zealand Women's Studies Association. This unique collection brings together a range of critical current texts from scholars working in both the humanities and social sciences. It provides an excellent illustration of the breadth and depth of research interests – particularly in issues of representation and identity – in the Pacific.

Place

For readers in the Northern hemisphere, the islands of the South Pacific often seem 'far away' both geographically and culturally. For those of us in the Pacific, forced to engage intimately with the Northern/Western intellectual, economic and political 'centre', that distance takes on different meaning. One is that we must explain ourselves: in this introduction we will at least remind the reader of the geographical location which we have taken as our 'umbrella' in this collection. The islands of the South Pacific include Aotearoa/New Zealand to the south, and the main centres of Samoa, Tonga and Fiji to the north. It is from these very different places that the authors of the articles in this book come; most are indigenous women, some are from families who were settlers in this region.

While we use the term 'Pacific' to indicate our geographic location, this phrase is not always used to describe the peoples in this region. Although of Polynesian descent, the indigenous people of Aotearoa/New Zealand, the Māori, are not usually considered 'Pacific Islands' people – nor are the Pākehā or Palagi. In New Zealand, where many people of the islands of Polynesia now reside, immigrants from the Pacific are often called by the increasingly popular gloss term 'Pacific Islands' peoples; elsewhere in the Pacific region they regain their cultural particularity as Samoan, Tongan, Fijian and so on.

The writers in this collection are Māori, Samoan, Samoan/Tuvaluan, Palagi, and Tongan. Like 'Pacific Islands', 'Māori' also acts as a homogenising term, disguising significant iwi (tribal) affiliations and differences within Aotearoa. Homogenisation also inheres in the terms 'Palagi', or 'Pākehā' – which are Samoan and Māori terms respectively for white settlers or peoples in this region. It is worth noting that the effects of these ethnic gloss terms are uneven. An aspect of Māori and Pacific peoples' experience of racism in Aotearoa is their collective and simplistic homogenisation, between and within those labels, in dominant group discourse – an effect not usually suggested by the local gloss terms for the white settlers.[3] Of course, any simple geographic or ethnic label fails to signal the range of contradictions of modern life and identity for many in the Pacific – contradictions exacerbated by the huge contemporary movements between and within the towns and cities of New Zealand and the home island states, or iwi regions.

Language

While the chapters in this book are written in English, readers will notice the hybrid nature of its language. The form of English used in Aotearoa/New Zealand commonly incorporates a number of Māori and some Samoan and Tongan terms which have come to be part of everyday English speech. Similarly in other parts of the Pacific, English usage is often characterised by the natural addition of terms from the indigenous languages. The question of how to present unfamiliar words to an English-speaking audience outside the Pacific becomes a political one. We resist making local languages of the South Pacific strange by italicising and including bracketed translations in the text. Hence, we have provided a list of translations in the form of a glossary on pages 9 and 10. We especially thank Te Kawehau Hoskins for her advice and help with compiling the Māori language glossary, and Lonise Tanielu for her work on the Samoan glossary.

Writing it

In this volume, *Jacqui Sutton Beets* examines the early twentieth century imaging of Māori women in tourist postcards. The postcard craze was certainly popular, with nine million cards being sent in 1909 alone. Although excluded from earlier written descriptions of Aotearoa/New Zealand, Māori women were visually portrayed in a number of stereotypical stock poses which had much to do with positioning them as exotic 'others' and very little to do with representing their lives. Sutton Beets identifies and discusses the posing of Māori women as 'the keepsake beauty', the degrading 'joke', 'Eve the tempted', 'Eve the temptress', 'mother and child', 'the noble savage' and as figures in 'authentic' ethnographic scenes from Māori village life. In all these 'poses', the underlying themes of exoticism, sexual availability and primitivism were manufactured for the voyeuristic white male gaze.

Te Kawehau Clea Hoskins writes of the complexities of Māori women's identity and Māori feminism within the Māori political struggle for Tino Rangatiratanga. Contextualised within the discourse of cultural heritage, Hoskins' elegant analysis considers the dialectical gendered politics surrounding notions of 'tradition', 'authenticity', 'sovereignty' and 'identity'. She considers the complex damage which colonisation has wrought, and continues to enact, on Māori and how this has affected the development of the Māori renaissance. The gendered reconstruction of a traditional society is problematised and made contemporary in a fresh discussion of Māori women's speaking rights on the marae. Hoskins analyses the basic tenets of white feminism and sets this against the politics of cultural reclamation and identity for Māori women.

Through a powerful first person narrative, *Lonise Tanielu* traces her ambivalent experiences of Samoan schooling. From her earliest memories of 'sitting still, keeping quiet, listening carefully, speaking out only when asked and being rewarded with the stroke of the stick or broom for misbehaviour' in the classroom to the importance of the Church and family in village life and the joys of youthful play, Tanielu evokes the bitter sweet essence of growing up female in Samoa. She continues this ambivalent theme in relaying her achievements in tertiary education: not always sweet, but certainly not always bitter. Her struggles and achievements provide an insight into growing up in Samoa with strong bonds to tradition and equal commitment for positive transformation in the face of modernity.

The vexed subject of sexual behaviour and identity among young Samoan women is the subject of *AnneMarie Tupuola*'s chapter. Fa'aSamoa (the Samoan way), fa'aloalo (respect) and ava (reverence) as well as the fear of disapproval and lack of privacy all contribute to a silence surrounding sexuality. Tupuola deals directly with the hesitancy and resistance to open discussion of these themes in the Samoan community, both in Samoa and in Aotearoa/New Zealand. Tupuola analyses the paradoxical, and sometimes conflicting, position of young women of Samoan descent with regards to their sexuality. She effectively accomplishes this by allowing the voices of young women themselves to speak. The result is a powerful and moving statement of young Samoan womanhood.

Jacqueline Leckie writes of the economic plight of the women in Fiji after the coup. She examines the political and economic upheavals of globalisation, colonialism, independence and the political coups of 1987 through the work experiences of three women of Fiji. The first, 'Mele', of indigenous Fijian-middle class descent, trained and worked as a nurse until the age of compulsory retirement. 'Asena', also of indigenous Fijian descent, but of lower economic status, lived in a village setting of rural Fiji until she and her husband migrated to Suva to find work in the export garment industry. The third, 'Sita', of Indo-Fijian descent, lives on a sugar cane farm with her husband and children. In a detailed analysis, Leckie examines the local as well as international forces that have direct bearing on the lives of these women of Fiji.

The image of Pacific Island women as an 'erotic', 'exotic' 'Other' is examined by *Tamasailau Suaalii* in her chapter. Suaalii uses a wide range of sources, including fine art, postcards, *National Geographic* and tourism literature, to explore how dominant Western views are employed in defining and constructing notions of Pacific Island beauty. Suaalii contextualises the representation of Pacific Island women under the guises of 'tourist exotic', 'exotic as occult' and 'exotic as pornographic'. Edward Said's *Orientalism* is employed in analysing these definitions and notions as representations of white, heterosexual male desire. Suaalii concludes with a consideration of the reclamation of this exotic imagery by Pacific Island women artists and fashion designers in co-opting an identity from the inside which was previously imposed from outside.

Judith van Trigt presents the construction and representation of the Pacific and Pacific Island women in five films, or cinematic texts: *Moana: A Romance of the Golden Age, South Pacific, Hawaii, The Bounty* and *Rapa Nui*. She analyses plot, dialogue and camera positioning in the context of the Pacific as 'Other' in Western subjectivities. Trigt argues that the West is preoccupied with the 'Other' (in this case the Pacific) as a means of supporting the gendered and racialised status quo of power relations and in defining itself against this 'Other'. The films give a good, albeit American, historical spread from the silent 1926 *Moana* to the 1994 *Rapa Nui*; although Trigt sees very little change in the dominant cinematic discourse over time. The Pacific is presented in terms of savageness, remoteness and as a 'Paradise under threat', while Pacific Islands women are continually constructed as silent, different and sexually available.

Examining the imprisonment of Māori women through the analytic lens of colonisation is the theme of *Helene Connor*'s chapter. Connor makes a connection between the high rate of imprisonment of Māori (both men and women) and an excoriation of Māori identity through over a century of Pākehā (Western) colonisation. The themes of identity and colonisation are interwoven with a consideration of imprisonment both literal (the actual numbers of Māori women incarcerated) and metaphorical (the 'capturing' of Māori women by British imperialism). As part of her consideration of metaphorical incarceration, Connor considers British notions of ideal womanhood and their impact on indigenous women through colonisation. Connor concludes her chapter by examining the contemporary identity politics of Mana Wāhine Māori and its potential in the reclamation of Māori women's lives lost through literal and metaphorical imprisonment.

Selina Tusitala Marsh considers the poetic writing of Pacific Island women. From the 1973 launch of *Mana*, an indigenous literary publication, Marsh catalogues the contribution of women to contemporary Pacific Island colonial and post-colonial literature. Marsh then focuses on the work of four influential poets: Jully Makini, Grace Molina, Momoe Malietoa Von Reiche and *Konai Helu Thaman* whose exquisite poetry appears in this volume. Makini is from the Solomon Islands, Molina from Vanuatu, Von Reiche from Western Samoa and Thaman from Tonga. Marsh discusses the colonial and postcolonial concerns of the authors, the inherent differences in the Melanesian/Polynesian context, their relation to worldwide post-colonial literature and, importantly, why and from where the women write. It is in their shared experiences of racism, colonialism, independence and sexism that Marsh demonstrates the capacity and power of their writing.

Our inevitable collective location 'within' the colonial history of this region means that there are still far too few indigenous women scholars in the position to write and publish research in the Pacific. Many do not care to write in the manner demanded by the market-driven publishing environment, or in the style required by models of academic writing. Many others are engaged in the urgencies of everyday life, and its political struggles. Those who speak in this book do not address directly the significance of indigenous-ness, but all write out of a sense of place – in this case the Pacific. All are connected by their sharp view of women's lives in this complex site of both belonging and struggle.

Notes

1 See Selina Tusitala Marsh's discussion of Molisa's work in Chapter 10.
2 bell hooks, *Outlaw Culture: Resisting Representations.* (Routledge, New York/London, 1994), and Linda Tuhiwai Smith, *Decolonising Methodologies: Research and Indigenous Peoples.* (University of Otago Press, Dunedin, 1999).
3 Melani Anae, 'Towards a New Zealand-born Samoan identity: Some reflections on "labels"'. *Pacific Health Dialog*, Sept. 4:2 (1997), pp. 128-37.

ONE

Images of Māori Women in New Zealand Postcards after 1900

JACQUI SUTTON BEETS

In early twentieth century New Zealand, the buying, sending and collecting of postcards reached craze proportions. In the year 1909 alone, nine million cards travelled through the postal system – an astonishing amount of card mail to be generated by a population of just one million people.[1] This craze fully commercialised photography in New Zealand; photographic companies, such as Burton Brothers of Dunedin, made their fortunes out of it. Representations of indigenous Māori quickly became popular subjects for these cards, as they had been for nineteenth century *cartes de visite*, and postcard images of Māori continue to fill tourist centre kiosks in New Zealand in the 1990s. Representations of Māori women in particular have held wide appeal throughout the century. Just what that appeal consisted of, and in which guises the Māori female has been presented to the popular imagination through postcards, are the topics which will be examined in this essay.

The colonial postcard is a 'poor man's phantasm', producing cheap pseudo-knowledge of a colony and its women, both of which are presented as exotic and alluring.[2] Such 'knowledge', however, comes via a photographer's manipulation of staged model, set and props, and is merely a simulacrum of the reality it purports to represent.[3] The end result is a calculated redundancy of the native woman into a commercial object, created under the veil of aesthetic or ethnographic representation. It has been noted that prior to the escalation of tourism and commerce in New Zealand, Māori women seldom featured in Pākehā records.[4] As a tourist drawcard, however, photographic depictions of native women could easily project an image of magical allure and escape which would, with luck, 'rub off' on the visitor.[5] For those not visiting but settling, the postcard posited the suggestion of pleasurable ownership of a native woman and her land. Thus the postcard altered the Māori woman's status from invisibility to an array of commercial images which varied according to popular Western taste.

The majority of the postcards examined here are representative examples selected from the Ephemera Collection and other collections held at the Alexander Turnbull Library, and date from the 'craze' era of the early 1900s. Images of Māori women in these postcards fall into four broad categories: the lone female or maiden, presented in a variety of genres; pairs of Māori females; mother-and-child images; and group photographs, including formal portraits and representations of 'village-life'.

Among the most widely-distributed of early twentieth-century postcards were representations of 'Māori maidens', which drew inspiration from and followed on from nineteenth century photography and portraiture by artists such as Goldie and Lindauer. The majority of these images were posed, half-length 'portrait-style' photographs. The 'keepsake beauty' figure, commercialised in nineteenth century fashion-setting periodicals such as *Heath's Book of Beauty* (1833-47), was a favourite variation on the Māori maiden theme. Keepsake beauties represented a feminine ideal, usually aristocratic and possessing a standard physiognomy of large eyes, flowing dark hair, olive (not black) skin, dainty nose, oval jaw, and an all-over fragile look expressed by a sweet, passive, vulnerable gaze.[6] Figure 1 ('A Māori Maid, Rotorua, New Zealand' *circa* 1915) is a stereotypical 'keepsake'. Posed before a background of flax bushes, this model has been selected not for any distinctive 'Māori' features, but because she conforms to a particular European taste in female representation. Her fine-boned (thus presumably aristocratic and European) facial structure and pale skin bring her qualities of 'Otherness' (black hair, dark eyes and native costume) within boundaries of desirability acceptable to the Pākehā male voyeur. It is interesting in this context to note a nineteenth century traveller's impression of certain (though not all) Māori women:

> *1864* This settlement has always been famed throughout Māori land for the beauty of the women . . . during our stay we saw a few girls with complexions like southern gypsies, just fair enough to let the warm colour show through clear olive skin, and large dark lustrous eyes, with great ever-changing expression, and beautiful, snow-white, regular teeth.[7]

Keepsake beauties were commonly placed against exotic or romantic landscape backgrounds (in Figure 1, native vegetation) to evoke an image of a bygone era of pastoral simplicity. A similar nostalgic fantasy regarding primitive Māori life and untouched land filled the minds of many New Zealand colonists. The virgin bush depicted in Figure 1 carries obvious symbolic connotations of innocent desirability, readily displaced onto the female model by the postcard's viewer.

'Innocent' Māori belles were thus designed to appear erotically alluring; indeed, their 'innocence' is part of that allure. To the Pākehā male it is the wahine's lack of civilised education and/or corruption by civilisation which determines, as much as her race, her 'Otherness'. Because innocence is perceived as a desirable state, the native woman represents the 'good Other' which attracts rather than repulses.[8] Yet this good attraction cannot be divorced from its erotic undertone. By her gaze – looking directly and openly at the viewer – and costume (alluring bare flesh only temporarily screened by fibrous cloak and flax bush), Figure 1's model advertises the availability of a 'natural' and therefore guiltless

Figure 1: 'A Maori Maid, Rotorua, New Zealand'
Ephemera Collection, Alexander Turnbull Library, Wellington.

Figure 2: 'A Maori Lily'
Ephemera Collection, Alexander Turnbull Library, Wellington.

sexuality. Thus the erotic element present in such postcards is permissible precisely because it is 'Othered'.

Such Māori maiden images could be capitalised on as colonial 'humour'. This is seen in Figure 2 ('A Māori Lily'), an exotic belle image which shows clearly the extent to which postcard captions were employed to shape a viewer's interpretation.[9] This model's cloak has been 'artistically' arranged to display the maximum amount of upper torso permissable on a commercial (that is, non-pornographic) postcard, and her unsmiling face expresses a misery and bewilderment which is scarcely surprising when other elements in this photographic 'joke' are examined. Accorded central focus is a huge white lily, awkwardly grasped in the model's hand. This Western art icon dates back to medieval representations of the Virgin Mary, when both the flower and its colour symbolised innocence and purity. 'A Māori Lily', however, is presented as a parody of the pale, slender virgins of traditional iconography. Disregarding the fact that the ideal Māori woman *was* big, buxom and graceful, this model is presented to Pākehā eyes as clumsy and coarse;[10] her large, dark body, costumed to appear less than innocent, suggests the stereotypically-available indigenous woman. Because such a 'joke' exists only between the Pākehā photographer and the postcard's buyer/viewers, the model's true 'innocence' lies in her ignorance; although not expected to understand the scenario's innuendoes, her expression nevertheless suggests a baffled awareness of degradation.

Such photographic 'humour' was not confined to the early years of this century. Figure 3 shows a modern, coloured postcard, undated but probably produced after 1970. The caption reads: 'Māori maid in traditional costume admires waterlilies at Paradise Valley, Rotorua'. Again the viewer's focus is directed towards a lily, which in late nineteenth century European art had become a dualistic icon suggesting not only innocence but also 'thoughts of sin'; to an artistically-educated mind 'one condition of being ceaselessly suggest[ing] its opposite'.[11] The lush fern-and-stream setting is reminiscent of that Western mythical 'Paradise', the Garden of Eden, and thus this Māori maiden becomes an innocent Eve; bare limbs are revealed beneath her parted hair and flimsy garment. The lily she plucks presumably suggests her 'fall' from sexual innocence; the Fall of Mankind has commonly been depicted in art and literature in terms of sexual shame. A frog (probably a photographer's plastic prop) is positioned near Eve's ear; its green, serpent-shaped head appears to whisper temptations to her. This scenario calls to mind the image in Milton's *Paradise Lost* of Satan in frog-form, 'Squat like a Toad, close at the ear of Eve'.[12] Represented here, therefore, is a soft primitivist ideology which depicts indigenous Pacific peoples as the inhabitants of a (transient) Paradise or Golden Age.[13] Around a New Zealand place-name a photographer has constructed a 'joke' which only those educated in European theological and literary traditions can appreciate, 'humour' which subtly emphasises the presumed sexual proclivity of the Māori maiden.

Figure 3: 'Maori maid in traditional costume admires waterlilies at Paradise Valley, Rotorua'
Colour View Productions/National Publicity Studios. (Supplied courtesy of J. Muirhead's collection.)

Figure 4 (*facing page*): 'The Arawa Belle'
Quartermaine Collection, Alexander Turnbull Library, Wellington.

From innocent Eve the Tempted to fallen Eve the Temptress, Māori women in early twentieth century postcards were frequently represented as fully-developed seductresses, wantonly-posed. Postcards carrying titles such as 'Māori Princess' indicate another instance of humorous or ironic captioning, as the fallen woman of literary tradition was seldom of noble birth. In one such example, a so-called 'Princess' with chin moko (images of women with moko, that symbol of a soon-to-vanish exotic past, were highly sought after by postcard collectors), leans towards the viewer, through a studio set of twisted tree branches which suggests the tree of (carnal) knowledge. Her bold smile, eye-contact with the viewer, bare arms and flowing hair clearly suggest unrestrained sexuality. Images such as these served to reinforce a generalised stereotype of native women as sexually liberated, and the colony as a newly-opened 'paradise' of enjoyments for the Pākehā male.

With this in mind, we turn to another popular postcard pose for Māori women borrowed from the canon of Western art: the reclining odalisque, emblem of the seductive courtesan or harem-woman. In an artistic tradition stemming from representations of Venus, Roman goddess of sexuality, through to nineteenth century French paintings of colonised Oriental women, the reclining odalisque is the stock image of the passive, sexually available female. Figure 4 ('The Arawa Belle') shows a young Māori odalisque, complete with bare shoulders, flowing locks, and hands positioned to emphasise the bust. The studio setting of carved and woven panels represents a meeting house interior, providing the

viewer with a vicarious 'insider's gaze' or intimate knowledge of the indigenous world, much as postcards of Algerian women purported to give the French colonist a glimpse into the fascinating forbidden world of the harem. Such vicarious voyeuristic images presuppose an intimacy in and over the observed society, creating a sense of superiority for the postcard owner.[14] The Arawa Belle (her title indicates the sophisticated French art and fashion heritage) reclines against piled-up tartan blankets, which strike an incongruous note in the primitive setting – a hint, perhaps, of the productive uses to which civilisation will turn the Belle's 'wild' land.

Māori maidens were, like the Arawa Belle, frequently represented holding weapons, such as the patu or the taiaha. While these props, together with traditional costumes and settings, can be seen as filling an ethnographic or historical function, the popularity of images of weapon-bearing females also suggests a less benign motive. Not only is the model reduced to the level of the artifacts surrounding her,[15] but the image of a nubile maiden clinging to the tools of bloodthirsty barbarism creates an aura of violent eroticism which may titillate the male viewer. Both savagery and sexual freedom were popular stereotypes applied to the indigene.[16]

Such representation of native women as erotic beings, sexually available to the male colonist's gaze, fills three purposes. First, the temptation and guilt arising from erotic desire is conveniently transferred from the white male viewer onto the Other, the sensually-presented Māori female. Second, the possession of the indigenous woman is equated to possession of the colony's land. This is made clear in postcards of alluring Māori maidens positioned against backdrops of majestic caves, native bush or thundering waterfalls, or placed beside Māori carvings or the gateway to a Pā (signifying the culture of the past). A popular postcard genre produced in the early 1900s included the words 'Māoriland' or 'Kia Ora' formed from a photographic montage of Māori maidens and natural scenery. One such card depicts a sketch-map of the colony and an inset photograph of a Māori belle, with the printed caption: 'As you cannot come to New Zealand I send it on to you.' For *it*, read *her*. The maiden, representative of nature (either unspoiled or wild) invites the colonial gaze to penetrate, and consequently possess, both herself and her land.

Third, the sexual availability of the native woman connotes the absence of an aggressive native male society. When the male is defeated, the indigenous female is offered or offers herself as a metaphorical war trophy for the white victor.[17] Postcards produced in the early twentieth century rarely depict a Māori maiden accompanied by a protective Māori male. An exception is the family group, such as a popular studio portrait titled 'Group of Otago Māoris' (produced *circa* 1904). In this representation, the subjects (possibly grandfather, father and daughters, or mother and daughter) wear cloaks and carry ceremonial weapons. Any Māori family possessing the financial resources and Western tastes to sit for its photograph – itself an interesting reversal of power-roles between Pākehā photographer and Māori subject – would have been likely also to possess quality Western clothing. That their representation in *traditional* costume should be selected for commercial postcard use indicates the ideology of Māori whānau, with stern warriors protecting its females, being a phenomenon of the past, not the present.

Another popular nineteenth century stereotype of the indigene was that of the 'noble savage' or 'romantic savage'. Postcards frequently depicted such figures: one entitled 'A Rangatira Māori' is a representative example. In this card the subject, a middle-aged female with chin moko, is costumed in cloak and patu; her facial expression is noble and determined, and her luxuriant hair flowing from beneath a scarf, aristocratic bone-structure, and resilient grasp of the traditional weapon combine to create an impression of a folkloric gipsy queen, the proud and warlike remnant of a dispossessed people. Such depictions of a woman of menopausal age dressed in traditional costume subtly signify a culture which can be no more; the nubile maiden, on the other hand, represents prime potential for intermarriage and assimilation.

Postcard images of maidens and noble savages were frequently idealised but could also suggest a purposely 'ethnographic' flavour, such as the rural 'village group'. One such image depicts three Māori women of indeterminate age, wearing cloaks and holding taiaha, positioned in front of a meeting house. The combined elements of such scenes (dark skin, ceremonial costumes, weapons and primitive architecture) purported to fulfil an historical function; in reality, they satisfied the European appetite for the exotic, the curious and the bizarre. Again the viewer is permitted the thrill of vicariously penetrating the unknown world of the meeting house. Such representations fill a similar function to the 'tourist romance' films of the 1920s and 1930s, providing primitivistic 'oases of timelessness' which confirm the chronopolitics of a civilising mission, relegating Māori culture to a nostalgic past.[18] In the same vein, tourist postcards throughout the twentieth century show Māori women performing picturesque poi dances and action songs in pseudo-traditional concert-party clothing. Like stereotypical Middle Eastern dancing girls, these bare-armed performers have become, in accordance with Pākehā taste, an indispensable part of the colonialist repertoire of indigenous images.[19]

Postcards of famous female tourist-site guides such as Rangi, Sophia, and the 'twin guides', Georgina and Eileen, also achieved popularity throughout the twentieth century. In these, Māori women are represented both as tokens of an exotic, primitive past, and as angelic guides, ushering the European male through a gateway into an elusive (lost or vanishing) and escapist Other-world that can be reached only through them. Occasionally however postcards representing female Māori guides emphasised an ideology of civilising European values. An early twentieth century example depicts '"Kathleen", Māori Guide,

Rotorua, N.Z.'. This bust-length portrait of a young woman, demurely attired in high-necked blouse, bonnet and jacket decorated with lace and flowers, creates an initial impression of Edwardian femininity epitomised. Although 'Kathleen's' expression (half-smiling and gazing away from the viewer) is respectful, decorous and 'civilised', her dark hair and skin, tiki ornament and tukutuku panel backdrop identify her racially as Māori, as do the inverted commas surrounding her European name. (This Anglo-Irish name is interesting, suggesting simultaneously the rural charm of the Gaelic maiden – the plant 'Kathleen' toys with appears to be a variety of shamrock – and the British Empire's successful colonising mission in areas other than the Pacific.) Such interrelated Western and Māori elements point to a subtext of colonial assimilationist policies: 'Kathleen' is presented as an example of the once savage native female who has absorbed civilised values – though, according to the inverted commas, this process may be only partially completed.

The native woman who repents of savagery and turns for salvation to the great white god of civilisation is frequently depicted on New Zealand photographic postcards. Several examples exist (with captions such as 'Meditation') of images not dissimilar to Renaissance representations of Mary Magdalene. In Western art, this subject was frequently depicted in a contradictory way, emphasising the repentant woman's flesh instead of her soul, an example being Titian's 'The Penitent Magdalene' (*circa* 1533) in which the subject is clothed only in her own hair.[20] Free-flowing hair, an erotic fetish in Victorian art,[21] was used to effect on postcards of partly 'civilised' Māori maidens, together with the strategic arrangement of bare arms and shoulders, and a bland, inward-looking gaze suggesting moral contemplation. As well as Māori Magdalenes, Māori Madonnas made popular postcard themes. Examples exist of typical Virgin Mary-like poses with the model modestly cloaked (although a glimpse of flesh usually remains revealed for the viewer's enjoyment). The subject's distant gaze and pensive expression create an impression of innocence and timelessness similar to that found in traditional paintings of the Virgin. Both Madonna and Magdalene poses represent the wild native woman as sanitised for European consumption, her 'natural' innocence translated to the moral purity of the Christian saint. Such 'innocence', however, probably created less than saintly overtones in the male Pākehā viewer's mind.

Following on from Madonna poses, mother-and-child portraits were popular postcard subjects, influenced by the famous Lindauer portraits of Ana Rupene and her baby.[22] Such photographs frequently focused on the method of carrying babies high on the back and were accompanied by such captions as 'How a Māori Carries Her Piccaninny. N.Z.', thus identifying the Māori woman, even in her universal maternal role, as 'Other'. These images were designed to be either sentimental and charming, using a young attractive mother and cute child as models, or ethnographic in purpose – a glimpse into 'old Māori ways'.

Many other so-called 'ethnographic' representations of daily Māori life were reproduced on postcards in the early twentieth century. A common misconception among Europeans steeped in chronopolitics was that the Māori was a dying race. Traditional indigenous societies were also considered somehow 'purer' than the resulting colonial hybrid and traditional life had presumably therefore to be documented as rapidly as possible.[23] Postcard representations of the 'old ways' included both posed compositions and what appear to be snapshots of village hapū or extended family groups taken on 'ethnographic' photographic tours throughout rural areas. To these were added such captions as 'Their First Photograph: Māoris on the Wanganui River' or 'In the Ngawhas, "Whaka-rewarewa", the most unique Māori picture ever taken.' Photographs of topless women bathing, in particular, were highly sought after and increasingly hard to come by in the moralistic post-missionary era.[24] In these cases, captions with ethnographic-sounding titles apparently pasted a respectable 'authentic' veneer over the voyeuristic nature of the subject.

Representations of village life also included images of Māori children, ranging from the cute, large-eyed waifs popular in Victorian and Edwardian photographic portraiture to the comic 'Penny Haka' genre, which depicted boisterous youngsters eager to show off for a fee. One such postcard (titled 'A Haka for a Penny, Rotorua') borders on 'coon humour': barefoot, ill-clad children gesture and grimace in a parody of the traditional war dance. Like similar representations of American Blacks and the Australian Aborigine in the early twentieth century, such images helped foster stereotypes of Māori as racially inferior simpletons.[25] The girls and boys whose images appear in these cards have been exposed at an early age to the Pākehā perspective of Māori. The 'Haka for a Penny' children present to Western eyes the degenerate post-colonial Māori, who regards ancestral traditions as commercial commodities to be traded for a ridiculously scant sum. These little urchins, who dress in ill-fitting and mis-matched Western clothes and prefer bare feet to warm, hygienic footwear, are presumably representative of the indigene who is unwilling or unable to appreciate the values of assimilation.

In contrast, the child-waif or huge-eyed, bare-shouldered gamine, represented in postcards with titles such as 'Startled', is presented as already filling the role of native woman assigned to her by a colonial hegemony: that of attractive vulnerable object, posed against a background of symbolic primal vegetation and offered for the delectation and possession of the European male.

Some postcard photographers concentrated on particularised images of rural Māori women engaged in domestic activities, including communal cooking, weaving, and washing clothes in rivers or tubs, in accordance with the ethnographic view of native women as repositories of traditional ways and values.[26] In these cards (with captions such as 'Māori Kitchen, Whaka-rewarewa'), Māori females are not idle reclining belles but hard-working drudges, 'ignorant and enslaved by ... labour'.[27] The women and children wear second-hand European clothes and blankets, and their living conditions (hinted at by background settings of primitive wooden huts, miscellaneous tin utensils, sacks over a hāngi, and clothing items draped across fences) are clearly substandard in comparison to contemporary European dwellings. In fact, many rural Māori prior to 1940 did live in 'substandard' dwellings without indoor kitchens, running water or toilets.[28] Some Westerners were inclined to view such lack of hygiene as 'the result of moral and cultural decline rather than economic hardship, social inequalities and the policies of successive governments';[29] postcard images of 'Māori kitchens' therefore reinforced a negative stereotype of the indigene as dirty and ineducable.

The representation of old women or kuia in early postcards likewise owes much to a prevailing cultural ideology of Māori facing an unwelcome civilising influence. Images of kuia smoking pipes, with captions such as 'Kapai te Torori (Tobacco is Good)' were modelled after famous Goldie portraits of the same genre, such as the popular 'Darby and Joan' (1903). The subject of one postcard in this genre (significantly titled 'Thinking of bygone days') wears a cloak decorated with ragged feathers. Her mop of white hair is uncombed, and her face, backlighted to accentuate its mass of wrinkles, is tilted downwards, eyes closed, in a sorrowful, musing expression. The composition is carefully arranged – against a dark background, a carved Māori representation of a human face appears to look down on the subject in pity – and the postcard's caption neatly sums up the popular misconception of Māori as a dying race, with a calculated combination of sentiment and irony.

A widely-held racial stereotype in the nineteenth and early twentieth centuries was that black peoples (especially females) were pathologically predisposed to sexual immorality.[30] The 'scientific' conclusions of Social Darwinism helped to firmly establish these stereotypes in the popular mind.[31] For instance, Saartje Baartman, the so-called 'Hottentot Venus', was toured throughout Europe as a living model of racial sexual anomaly and, after her death, her autopsied genitals and famous protruding buttocks were displayed at Paris's Musée de l'Homme. It is in this context that we examine the 'coon humour' of postcards such as Figure 5 ('Kiss Me'). The 'comic savage',[32] subject of this Trevor Lloyd caricature, wears the cloak, moko, tooth earring and hair feather of an alluring Māori belle, but her flat nose and thick lips are stereotyped negroid features, while her puckered mouth and rolling eyes signify a gross and unbridled sexuality. The card is presented as a generalisation of the presumed pathological sexual disposition of Māori females; again, a brand of 'humour' amusing only to the Pākehā male viewer.

Another significant postcard representation of Māori women is that of 'twins': such images often depict two females embracing or performing the hongi, with a caption such as 'Loving Sisters' or 'A Māori Kiss'. Paintings of

Figure 5: 'Kiss Me'
Ephemera Collection, Alexander Turnbull Library, Wellington.

languid females draped around each other were popular in late Victorian art; these lesbian-like couples provided males with images of erotic desire which made no personal demands upon the voyeur.[33] Representations similar to (although often more pornographic than) these Māori 'twins' appeared on Algerian colonial postcards, revealing the French colonist's fascination with the imagined sexual excesses of the harem (including sapphism). Such cards conveyed a generalisation that all native women were sexually perverted and/or lascivious.[34] 'Loving Sisters' and 'Māori Hongi/Salutation/Kiss' images therefore appealed to the voyeuristic male postcard collector who, basing his judgements of behaviour on the mores of Western culture, imputed erotic overtones to the hongi.

Māori women made picturesque, accessible and malleable subjects for the colonial photographer. With little idea of the motives behind the camera lens, these women submitted themselves to the Pākehā patriarchal gaze, to be costumed, posed, photographed, captioned, distributed and possessed. As such they unknowingly presented to and reinforced in the Western mind a canon of stereotypes about themselves: sexually inviting and/or immoral; inherently violent; ignorant; either in a process of civilisation or unwilling to change and be successfully assimilated; a conquered and dying race. New Zealand postcards featuring Māori women thus suggest a policy of exploitation by early twentieth century recorders and image-makers, males 'who strove to capture a deliberately ambiguous image'.[35]

Through the exceedingly popular medium of commercial postcards, colonialist, sexist and racist ideologies became engrained in the public mind. To overseas postcard recipients, representations of New Zealand and its indigenous women such as those discussed here offered a presumably 'accurate' record of colonial experience; in many cases, the only record to which the viewer had access. For the New Zealand postcard buyer, sender or collector, the cards (constantly on display at post offices and public kiosks) reinforced an ideology of Māori women as stereotypes: urchin, maiden, drudge; nubile belle or dying kuia. As for their overseas recipients, for many urban Pākehā the cards may have provided their only knowledge of Māori women and rural native life in the early decades of this century.

Represented on popular postcards, Māori women, their land and their culture are reduced by patriarchal mechanisms to the level of commercial prostitution. As a prostitute is a woman who fulfils a sexual-economic function while being controlled by males, models for these postcards become fallen women, lost in the sense of their ability to maintain individual and cultural integrity, and manipulated by a photographer-pimp and a buyer- or viewer-client.[36]

The study of postcard representations of Māori women is therefore of importance in terms of understanding gender and colonial relations in New Zealand. Such images as those discussed in this essay have helped to shape generations of popular thought in this country, for both Pākehā and Māori. As such, they represent part of the vast canon of calculated pictorial commodification of women, and women of colour in particular. These images therefore contribute to the racist and sexist attitudes which have persisted throughout the twentieth century, and which continue to challenge Māori women – and all women – today.

Notes

1   Michael King, *Maori: A Photographic and Social History* (Heinemann, Auckland, 1983), p. 2.

2   Malek Alloula, 'The Colonial Harem', trans. Myrna Godzich & Wlad Godzich in *Theory and History of Literature*, Vol. 21 (University of Minnesota Press, Minneapolis, 1986), p. 4.

3   Ibid., pp. 64, 68.

4   Ngahuia Te Awekotuku, *Mana Wahine Maori: Selected Writings on Maori Women's Art, Culture and Politics* (New Women's Press, Auckland, 1991), p. 77.

5   Haunani-Kay Trask, *From a Native Daughter: Colonialism and Sovereignty in Hawai'i* (Common Courage Press, Monroe, Maine, 1993), p. 180.

6   Leonard Bell, *Colonial Constructs: European Images of Maori 1840-1914* (Auckland University Press, Auckland, 1992), pp. 17-18.

7   Herbert Meade, quoted in Te Awekotuku, p. 90.

8   Sander Gilman, *Difference and Pathology: Stereotypes of Sexuality, Race and Madness* (Cornell University Press, London, 1985), p. 20.

9   Sarah Graham-Brown, *Images of Women: The Portrayal of Women in Photography of the Middle East 1860-1950* (Columbia University Press, New York, 1988), p. 2.

10 Te Awekotuku, p. 92.

11 Bram Dijkstra, *Idols of Perversity: Fantasies of Feminine Evil in Fin-de-Siècle Culture* (Oxford University Press, New York/Oxford, 1986), p. 191.

12 John Milton, *Paradise Lost*, ed. Christopher Ricks (Penguin, London, 1989), IV. 800, p. 100.

13 Bernard Smith, *European Vision and the South Pacific 1768-1850: A Study in the History of Art and Ideas* (Oxford University Press, London, 1960), pp. 25-7.

14 Alloula, p. 29.

15 Graham-Brown, p. 40.

16 Terry Goldie, *Fear and Temptation: The Image of the Indigene in Canadian, Australian and New Zealand Literatures* (McGill-Queens University Press, Kingston, 1989), p. 15.

17 Alloula, p. 122.

18 Martin Blythe, *Naming the Other: Images of Maori in New Zealand Film and Television* (The Scarecrow Press, Metuchen, New Jersey and London, 1994), p. 63.

19 Graham-Brown, p. 170.

20 John Berger et al., *Ways of Seeing* (BBC & Penguin, London, 1972), p. 92.

21 Bell, p. 143.

22 Ibid, p. 236.

23 Graham-Brown, p. 15.

24 King, p. 21.

25 Ibid, pp. 23-4.

26 Graham-Brown, p. 15.

27 Ibid., p. 145.

28 King, p. 75.

29 Graham-Brown, p. 108.
30 Gilman, p. 83.
31 Graham-Brown, p. 14.
32 Smith, p. 129.
33 Dijkstra, pp. 69-70.
34 Alloula, pp. 95, 103.
35 Te Awekotuku, p. 94.
36 Trask, pp. 185-191.

TWO

In the Interests of Māori Women?
Discourses of Reclamation

TE KAWEHAU CLEA HOSKINS

It is with both compulsion and trepidation that I have approached the writing of this chapter. Trepidation, because as a Māori woman, as an 'insider', it is not easy to speak critically about aspects of your culture, society or cultural practice without providing ammunition to a racist and fearful society, or risking personal attack and exclusion. Compulsion, because I believe profoundly that critique of all aspects of our cultural and political reclamation and reconstruction is imperative to forging a just, autonomous and inclusive future.

This discussion therefore is written as an 'insider' and is meant to promote discussion and reflection, for the most part 'internal' to the broad Māori struggle for Tino Rangatiratanga. As a Māori woman who seeks to contribute usefully to this struggle, I bring my own reflections and experiences to the discussion together with the greater experience, reflection and insight of other Māori women theorists, writers, artists and activists, all of whom inform and contribute to our struggles for liberation as Māori and as Māori women.

Focusing the Discussion

This paper is an attempt to engage with some of our current cultural discourses, particularly those which assert the reclamation and reconstruction of authentic, and traditional identities, roles and relationships. Versions of these discourses, I contend, are being produced and taken up within our political and cultural projects of reconstruction. I attempt an engagement with several issues which relate to both the tenability and desirability of such projects. Particularly, I want to make comment on the ways I believe the deployment of cultural discourses related to gender may be constructing, reconstructing and positioning Māori women in ways that ultimately work against their/our interests. Finally, I explore some aspects of the notion of Māori feminism/s, and the reasons I consider they are important, indeed central, to a political vision of equality for all Māori.

The impetus for much of the validation and revival of te reo and tikanga is sourced in an intensely political motivation by groups like Nga Tama Toa and individuals like Hana Te Hemara and Syd Jackson. Te reo and tikanga are understood by Māori as central to any meaningful reclamation and reconstruction of a distinct and 'authentic' identity as Māori. They are two inseparable elements whose revival is seen as the cornerstone to a whole and functioning people. They are recognised (especially te reo) as a largely unpolluted source of insight and knowledge into the thinking/world view of our tūpuna and therefore to a time and knowledge base undisturbed by the forces of colonialism. This knowledge is embodied in the language through the many forms of waiata and haka, in whaikōrero, karanga, tauparapara, whakatauaki, karakia pūrakau and pakiwaitara. It is from these kinds of sources that, for many Māori, it is believed we can retrieve and reconstruct an 'authentic' Māori identity/ies and cultural life.[1] Substantial time, energy and resources have been invested in the reclamation and institution of te reo as exemplified in Kohanga Reo, Kura Kaupapa, Wānanga Reo and Whare Wānanga Māori, to name a few. This focus is central, indeed primary to the reclamation of a positive identity as Māori and therefore our collective and individual wellbeing.

The Problem of Critique

The processes of colonisation have meant, for many Māori, an almost absolute severing from the fundamental elements of a collective identity/ies: Māori language, knowledges and cultural and community life. However, through the renaissance of Māori culture and language, and the efforts of many generations of our activists, there are a growing number of Māori who have a critical awareness about the physical loss and cultural damage colonisation has perpetuated against our people. The numbers of Māori who mobilised in opposition to the Fiscal Envelope are testimony to this.[2] These are Māori who are critical and suspicious of what are viewed as corrupting Pākehā/Western values, motives, and practices. Indeed, this is a sensible and logical defence and necessary form of resistance when we consider that colonisation is alive and well in Aotearoa today. However it is my experience that we are particularly reluctant to employ such critical ideas to those cultural discourses and practices seen to be sourced from within our culture, and which, in part, are informing our reconstructive work.

Because many of us lack/lacked a strong and positive sense of 'identity/ies' as Māori, that is, we may not have experienced lives informed and influenced by things Māori, we are naturally eager to gain knowledge, information and insight into our culture and to incorporate and apply that learning and knowledge within ourselves, our work and our lives. However as Kathie Irwin points out, because this knowledge is sourced in a world and time we know little about, we feel almost completely unable to be critical of it. Rather, we tend to accept and take up ideas about 'tradition', placing our trust in those keepers and interpreters of what is promoted as 'authentic', genuine Māori knowledge, practice and thought.[3]

We are also fearful, as Jenny Te Paa suggests: 'To be an "insider" and to be seen as critical of "your own" is to be exposed to accusations of treachery and disloyalty. It is to risk vilification, abuse and probable expulsion'.[4] Added to this you may be accused of not being a 'real Māori', not 'tūturu', or being a 'colonised-in-the-mind Māori', or for being 'anti-development', negative and destructive in a fragile reconstructive environment. While the development of critique as a central working tool for a sophisticated culture of resistance is essential to our struggle, so too is the encouragement and employment of these same tools within our reconstructive work and that which informs it. We must not risk rigid exclusions of useful and complementary ideas and knowledges, nor risk the inclusion of discourses which may inhibit the development of a method of self determination – a culture of liberation, for all Māori.

Authenticity and Reclamation

Discourses which assert the comprehensive retrieval of an 'authentic' and originary past are not currently in ascendancy in Māori 'development' models. However, it is significant that elements of these can be identified in many espousals of the 'way forward' for Māori. It is for this reason I would like to explore further notions of authenticity and reclamation. While I believe the instituting of structures sourced in the collectively identified values, principles and philosophy of our culture are essential to the wellbeing of our people and the continuation of our struggle for an autonomous future, the assumption that the path forward is the continuation or re-instituting of structures and tikanga believed to be traditionally *authentic* is problematic for at least two reasons. First, it assumes that this project of reclamation is possible, and second, that it is desirable.

From the first point of contact with tauiwi, our undisturbed sovereignty and cultural life and identities irrevocably changed. Like Linda Tuhiwai Smith, I believe that all our social structures have been 'colonised, distorted and rearranged' and that the modes of colonisation (warfare, disease, law) and the imposition of a distinctly Western hegemony, have meant the construction of 'new' forms of social (including gender), economic and political relationships both within Māori culture and between Māori and Pākehā.[5] We must remind ourselves that culture is dynamic and changing; Māori culture prior to colonisation was not static, nor obviously is it today. Our cultural life did not cease around 1769 or 1840, it was forced to negotiate the forces of colonialism and imperialism. It has been negotiating these forces and relationships ever since.

Discourses espousing an authentic reclamation are problematic too because they tend not to consider that, having internalised 160 years of colonial experience, it may be nigh impossible to retrieve and reconstruct the world view our tūpuna lived within. However 'de-colonised', however critical we believe ourselves to be, we cannot escape the immutable fact that our world is a vastly different place from that our tūpuna inhabited. Even in a relatively 'conscientised' condition, our consciousnesses are irretrievably changed/ changing in response to, and engagement with, the world/s we now inhabit. There is no clear space, free from the discourses which shape us, in which to attempt an 'authentic' reconstruction, as any reconstruction will inevitably be shaped at least in part by contemporary and historical discourses both from within Māori society and from 'outside'. This should not be considered a totally bad thing; an acknowledgment of it may relax or free-up the parameters of those discourses, creating gaps/spaces where our reconstructive work can draw from the obvious integrity of our value base while creating new and imaginative possibilities for the construction of tikanga/practice and structures consistent with our needs and aspirations today.

However, as Shohat points out, colonised communities are 'obliged by circumstances to assert, for their very survival, a lost and irretrievable past. In such cases, the assertion of culture prior to conquest forms part of the fight against continuing forms of annihilation'.[6] As many of us are aware, the defence of the legitimacy of our rights to culture and language are under constant attack, both from within Aotearoa and by colonising forces from outside. Clawing out and maintaining a space for their legitimacy, in which our children, mokopuna and ourselves can thrive, is an ongoing struggle. It is in this fear of risking continued annihilation that, I believe, we cling unquestioningly to certain cultural notions and practices. It is a powerful motivating force which has, in part, meant the retention of fragments of our knowledge base and world view. However, I would venture that it is imperative that we begin to promote the notion that tikanga are only tika – that is, they are only useful practices in the contemporary contexts to which they respond, and that change is absolutely necessary if tikanga are to be a central, meaningful guiding force within our society and not relegated to a solely ritualistic function.

Notions of authenticity within our reconstructive work can encourage and perpetuate negative binary distinctions and relationships, with their implied legitimacy and superiority, like tribal/urban, speaker of te reo/non speaker, tūturu/ born again, decolonised/colonised, dark/fair, full blooded/half caste. These kinds of distinctions perpetuate a narrow and oppositional world view. Our subordinate positioning within oppositional dualisms inherent in the colonising ethos is one we must be mindful not to reproduce within our own cultural reconstruction. These relationships have meant the censure of those less powerfully positioned, and for Māori to make such distinctions ignores and conceals the experience of colonisation, thereby further dehumanising those most dispossessed among us. Notions of authenticity which are politically motivated, and designed even in part to set in motion a hierarchy of power and legitimacy in the interests of those who articulate them, must be continually contested in the interests of a collective vision for all Māori.

Authenticity and Identity

'Post' colonial identity/ies for Māori, set within discourses of authenticity and reclamation, represent a search which, as Trinh T. Minh-ha suggests, is 'usually the search for a lost, pure, true, real, genuine, original, authentic self, often situated within a process of elimination of all that is considered other, superfluous, fake, corrupted or Westernized'.[7] I think many of us will recognise such assumptions informing our notions about the reclamation of an authentic, decolonised Māori identity. Trinh T. Minh-ha contends that this gives rise to the notion of the 'I' self as the authentic (Māori) self, and the 'other' as that part of oneself 'which is almost unavoidably either opposed to the self or submitted to the self's dominance'.[8] Identity understood this way supposes we are divisible, that we can mark out the authentic 'I' from the 'other'. As I earlier attempted to express, our identities are shaped and constructed by historical, social, political, and economic conditions and discourses; they are multiple and inexorably woven together. Where exactly is the place where I as a Māori leave off, and I as a Westernized, colonised, Pākehā take-up? However as Trinh.T Minh-ha also points out, 'This is not to say the historical I can be obscured and ignored and that differentiation cannot be made, but that I is not unitary,[and] culture has never been monolithic'.[9]

The notions of 'insider' and 'outsider' within the context of authenticity also become problematic. I have used the term 'insider' myself in self description as a way of defining my politics and loyalties as a Māori woman and in relation to the issues laid out in this chapter. However, I am always critically conscious that as a Māori woman in a 'post' colonial environment I am 'outsider' too. Colonisation has meant that I 'necessarily look in from the outside while also looking out from the inside. Not quite the same, not quite the other ... in that undetermined threshold place where [I] constantly drifts in and out'.[10] What is required for our reconstructive work as Māori is the development of and engagement with notions of identity which acknowledge and provide space for our multiplicity, our contradictions, and our difference as people, while at the same time affirming and encouraging our sameness.

Māori Women – Constructions of Place

Current cultural discourses informing our understandings of traditional gender relations also assert the retrieval of some, all, or aspects of those relationships as necessary to an 'authentic' reconstruction of ourselves as a people. As a point of clarification, my use of the word 'reconstruction' usually refers to the actual process of self determination, of defining and constructing appropriate models for the re-establishment of ourselves as an independent people. I am not usually referring to the process of reconstructing our past conditions through interrogation and research in order to inform the present, although of course they are related. Assertions for the reconstruction of traditional roles, do, in varying intensities, thread through our contemporary emancipatory discourses. They are problematic as they too assume such a task is both possible and desirable, and as with other notions considered genuine and authentic we are reluctant to be critical of them. Traditional gender discourses are also problematic, I believe, because their credibility contributes to the constructing of Māori women within cultural parameters which may ultimately work to our disadvantage. Shohat suggests that the question we must continue to ask is 'who is mobilising what in the articulation of the past, deploying what identities, identifications and representations, and in the name of what political vision and goals?'[11] This question must be asked of all discourses which inform and shape our reconstructive work.

Without question, Māori women have been/are constructed from 'outside' by Christian, colonial, Western, patriarchal discourse. Linda Smith, Leonie Pihama, Patricia Johnson, Kathie Irwin and many others, have written comprehensively about the marginalisation of Māori women through the destruction of our spheres and sites of power, and the imposition of colonial and Western ideologies of gender and race. As Leonie Pihama and Patricia Johnson articulate, this process has served to construct Māori women through the 'colonial gaze', locating us 'firmly within racist, and sexist ideologies', simultaneously as 'savages' and 'sexual objects'.[12] When we are not being referred to in this manner we are barely referred to at all, having been written out of history by Pākehā male writers and anthropologists, and made invisible by historical discourses. Linda Tuhiwai Smith contends that this process has included both the years after colonisation as well as before. This has not only obscured the diversity of roles enjoyed by Māori women, but made the task of accurately reconstructing our past conditions particularly difficult.[13]

It is certain however that some of us at least enjoyed powerful tribal leadership positions as exemplified within Ngāti Porou and other areas. We are able also to clearly identify strong female roles within our 'myth' traditions, and a multitude of identifiable female deities have survived as examples from which to draw strength. In contrast, as Leonie Pihama and Patricia Johnston point out, 'colonial ideologies pertaining to women located them as chattels, as the property of men, and therefore of lesser status',[14] yet according to Anne Salmond, in contradiction with much anthropological discourse, all Māori women enjoyed a better status than that being experienced by women in Europe at the time.[15]

The process of 'colonising, reorganising and distorting' our traditional gender roles has given rise to 'new' relationships,[16] like patriarchal or male bonding between Māori and Pākehā men. According to Leonie Pihama and Patricia Johnston, colonial rule meant that 'Pākehā men dealt with Māori men. The roles proffered for Māori women were mainly those of servitude....'[17] Kathie Irwin is also critical of these 'new' relationships which allow Pākehā/tauiwi 'men participatory rights in our culture over Māori women, simply because of their maleness'.[18] She argues that cultural change should logically advance the position of Māori women before Pākehā/tauiwi men.

Interrogating Gender Equality

Māori men within Māori society, I would argue, have largely become the legitimated keepers, interpreters and promoters of what is considered authentic, traditional knowledge and tikanga and kaupapa Māori. It is *they,* therefore, who are primarily articulating our past – in their own interests and political goals. However, Māori women too (perhaps as a strategic re-appropriation) are articulating certain cultural discourses, particularly those which assert the notion of complementary but equal traditional gender relations. For example, 'Māori Woman lived and drew her strength from the examples of her tūpuna wahine. Her presence and contribution was respected by the whole whānau, and accordingly she was granted material and power considerations equal to that of men'.[19]

It is significant that two of the Māori women writers of this quote hail from Ngāti Porou, an iwi renowned for the 'high' status their women enjoy/ed; indeed there is much evidence to support this claim provided by and for Ngāti Porou women. But, to suggest that this status was universally enjoyed by all Māori women, regardless of iwi or whakapapa/rank distinctions is, to my mind, unjustified idealism. Such assertions by Māori women may also, however, be read as counter discourses or discourses of resistance to those which have positioned us historically as downtrodden savages. Nevertheless, as Linda Tuhiwai Smith reminds us, 'Fundamental to Māori women's struggle to analyse the present has been the need to reconstruct [accurately] the past conditions of Māori women'.[20]

The popular notion of traditional gender complementarity – defined as different/separate spheres in work and social relations for women and men – does not, in my opinion, necessarily mean that 'material and power considerations' automatically flow to all Māori women. Indeed, patriarchally and Christian inspired missionary/coloniser-conveyed notions of gender role 'complementarity' were *not* about the sharing of decision making and power, but about separate roles with women clearly positioned as subservient to men. I do not assert that our gender relations simply mirrored those brought by the colonisers, rather I point to the problematic and largely uncritical use of this notion of complementarity as it is invoked as 'proof' of gender equality within our cultural discourse.

Matrilineality as it pertains to the practices of descent and the handing on of land is also, in my experience, often evoked as incontestable evidence of our equal status with men. Yet as Taiamoni Tongamoa points out, both these practices can sit comfortably within patriarchy and do not necessarily indicate women having status and power. She writes that:

> Female 'landowners' in that minority of Melanesian societies that are matrilineal, and those of Micronesia (most of which are matrilineal) do not necessarily have authority in the traditional decision making body, even about land. More accurately they do not hold the rights to the lands themselves, but they are the channel through which the rights to it are passed.[21]

Kate Millet has this to say on the subject: 'Matrilineality, which may be, as some anthropologists have held, a residue or a transitional stage of matriarchy ... does not constitute an exception to patriarchal rule, it simply channels the power held by males through female descent'.[22] While it is impossible to generalise very far about cultural patterns and practices, and it is essential that our culture is explained in the context of our society, Tongamoa's and Millet's observations broaden the scope for consideration and critique.

Grace Mera Molisa's writings are particularly useful to this discussion because as a Pacific Islands, indigenous woman, she offers a counter position on traditional gender relations to those in ascendancy here. Margaret Jolly paraphrases Grace Mera Molisa's position in this way:

> [She] does not claim that women were indigenously the equals of men, or that contemporary male domination is only the product of colonialism or that naming women's subordination is divisive to national unity ... and though suspicious of European feminism .... she does assert that many indigenous cultures of Vanuatu were male dominated, and that present problems represent a compounding of Melanesian and European misogyny and that women must struggle to keep the issues of gender on the agenda in the post colonial state (of Vanuatu).[23]

Grace Mera Molisa's thoughts open up this discussion to some of our own contemporary examples which could also be labelled misogynistic, but are more likely to be constructed within the discourse of Māori women's 'difference' to men, and notions of tapu and noa. As notions of tapu and noa are complex and involved, I raise them here only in relation to a specific example. One prevalent discourse asserts that all people have/are tapu – that is, sacred and subject to restriction – and that women have the additional 'power' of whakanoa, the ability to make things and situations clear and unrestricted. John Delamere's attack on Helen Clark for sitting on the 'paepae tapu' at Waitangi seems to evoke another discourse, which posits women as only noa, that is not tapu, and because of this condition, in need of restriction, in order to protect tapu.[24]

Delamere's comments construct noa, and by implication Māori women, as polluting or profane, as opposed to clear and unrestricted. In my experience, this notion (women as noa) has been largely 'disowned' within some quarters because it is considered to be influenced by Christianity and patriarchy, and because it does not fit within our notions of traditional gender equality. It is however, one that still persists within Māori society. Respected Tainui kaumātua

Te Uira Manihera writes that he instructed a young boy to take some whakapapa books, which had been handed down through his father, away from food and clothing that belonged to women. He writes: 'Knowledge that is profane has lost its life, lost its tapu'.[25] Food as a means to whakanoa, or to lift tapu, is commonplace in Māori society. However, the distinction made here between food belonging to women and that presumably belonging to men, seems to suggest that it is in its belonging to women – and, by inference, by women – that something can be made 'profane', or without life.

Delamere's remark that 'Te Arawa would not start proceedings with *her* or any other woman sitting on the speakers' bench' is in keeping with the view that women are indeed polluting beings.[26] He states the front bench is for 'speakers' and although Helen Clark as a woman did not transgress any tikanga by speaking, one can only assume that by virtue of being a woman (and noa) she polluted a tapu, male space. Is the 'paepae tapu' tapu because it is a male space, or because the act of whaikōrero, the words themselves and the entire ritual of encounter, are tapu? Would it follow that the karanga, as an essential element within the rituals of encounter and another form of speech on the marae, because it is performed by women, be considered noa? It is not surprising to most of us that Mr Delamere is a member of an iwi renowned for its rigidity about gender. It was also a contingent of Te Arawa men who went to parliament in 1933 for the express purpose of walking out when Elizabeth McCombs, the first woman MP, rose to give her 'Maiden' Speech.[27] A further example is Kathie Dewes' legal struggle to become a member of the Te Arawa Trust Board. On what 'tikanga' grounds could her exclusion be defended other than the misogynist belief that as a woman she is a lesser and polluting being?

It is examples like these which make our culture appear sexist in the extreme; can we continue to accept that the infiltration of Western beliefs can take all the credit? Whatever the source, we cannot allow the continuation of these kinds of practices, veiled and legitimated by the sanctity of culture, to go unchallenged. Although two of my examples here have related to Pākehā women (there are issues of race and power involved here, for example Helen Clark was given the opportunity to speak at Waitangi while Georgina Te Heuheu was ignored), I am acutely aware that it is Māori women who suffer most from these oppressive discourses and practices.[28]

Gender and the Marae

I would now like to focus for a time on the marae, a much discussed setting in terms of gender distinction. It is one area I have been able to find dissenting voices among Māori women on which to draw for this discussion. There has been much contestation and focus on the marae as a site of struggle for Māori women. Kathie Irwin points out that it is only Western notions of what constitutes speaking which fail to acknowledge women's karanga as a form of speech; from a Māori perspective, she contends, Māori women are not without power, status or voice on the marae.[29] While we might agree with Irwin's argument, Ripeka Evans questions why women's 'oratory' on the marae should be restricted to karanga. She states:

> The notion that female oratory should be restricted to rituals of encounter stems from a belief in a divine ordinance that the marae-atea belongs only to men. (This notion pervades practices and procedures which are entrenched in non-marae situations.) It is not just the debate about speaking rights on the marae which is the issue, but more the fuel which this powerful metaphor of restricted rights adds to Māori male hegemony – how it doubly oppresses and entrenches, how it silences and vaporises, how it extinguishes the collective voice of women.[30]

Ripeka Evans raises the issue of the silencing of women, not only on the marae but in many other Māori and non-Māori fora. Indeed, in my experience it is very rare to see women speak in formal proceedings held within the wharehui (although ideologically at least it is permitted), and it is with trepidation that many, especially younger Māori women, speak at all within the wharehui even in an 'open' forum, unless it is with a group with whom they are completely secure. As Ranginui Walker points out, in the many years he has spent time on marae around the North Island, only once has he seen a woman speak.[31] Yet the 'fact' that in a number of tribal areas in the North Island women are 'permitted' and do speak on the marae is held up by both Māori men and women as examples of our equal status with men. Rangi Walker's observations suggest that this notion is more an ideology than an actuality. The continued production and promotion of such notions which conceal the 'facts'/reality of Māori women's experiences serve to obscure or divert our recognition of them as such and hence escape challenge and the possibility of change.

Marae, in my experience, can be extremely unsafe places to be if you are a woman. I have been part of a group who have held Wānanga Reo at different marae around the country for the past five years and over that time I have questioned the wisdom of doing so many times. I have seen women stopped by men in the middle of their mihi and lectured on what a woman can and cannot, should and should not, acknowledge/speak of in her mihi. Not only is this kind of behaviour totally oppressive, but to the many, often impressionable, tauira who attend wānanga, this is an affirmation of male dominance and sets an example to Māori men and women that these kinds of behaviours are legitimate and acceptable in our culture. Mira Szaszy, a long time promoter of women's speaking rights on the marae has this to say:

> Our marae is a patriarchal institution, 'pervaded by assumptions of male domination'. This position of women in our political whānau mirrors the role of women in society. The custom which disallows women from speaking on that forum with the assertion that men and women have complementary roles is, in fact 'a denial of equality, as such roles are certainly not equal'.[32]

In recalling the establishment of the Māori Women's Welfare League, Szaszy speaks of the necessity 'to set up a structure which was not dominated by men, i.e. on non-Māori lines'. She goes on to note that marae structures were never brought into League conferences by Māori men at that time but that she has 'the powerful feeling that marae kawa has now followed us, intruding even into the house of the League'.[33] Mira Szaszy's observations implicate the last twenty or so years of cultural renaissance in the entrenching of the kawa of the marae in many other Māori and non-Māori fora. It is my opinion that, while it is an extremely difficult, dangerous and fraught process for women to assert ourselves on the marae, it must happen; and it is absolutely imperative that we 'take back' those many other fora in which Māori women are being silenced, from the domination of marae kawa and Māori male hegemony.

Recently a group of us held a national hui (off the marae) for people involved with decolonisation education work. Prior to the hui, we spent many hours discussing the ways in which we could transform the rituals of encounter to begin this hui and as group member Jacq Carter later wrote: 'we consciously sought, not simply to oppose or reverse the way in which these rituals are normally carried out, but to alter them in a way that satisfied us and our new "criteria" and met our collective aspirations in addressing the need for change'.[34] A female member of our group welcomed our manuhiri and then we opened the floor for mihi to be returned or introductions to be made by anyone. Interestingly, this departure from the normal conventions unnerved our manuhiri, who retreated to conservatism – only men spoke to return mihi or to introduce themselves. This was an example to us of how, even in a relatively informal environment, the kawa and hegemony of the marae culture has entrenched itself, and indeed has been so internalised by Māori women that the justification for not speaking in a non-marae forum is the 'chosen' adherence to our own marae and iwi kawa and tikanga. It also indicates that many Māori women have been denied the opportunity to gain the confidence to speak or indeed the confidence or belief that we may have anything meaningful to say.

In Whose Interests?

Māori women have for a long time been critical of notions of white feminism, and with good reason. Western feminist tradition has for a long time posited gender as the primary and universal site of oppression, while largely ignoring factors of class and race. To Māori women this position is untenable because it fails to expose/own/acknowledge not only white/Pākehā women as beneficiaries of Māori women's dispossession through colonisation, but also their continued implication in these relations in a 'post'-colonial Aotearoa. Our status as tangata whenua, our culture and shared experience of colonisation (with Māori men) situates Māori women in a much larger reality than that of 'women's rights'.[35] Indeed there is a fear that even in the more recent feminist acknowledgment and inclusion of 'other' women's voices/experiences/specificity, these too will be appropriated and assimilated into what Ien Ang describes as 'a new, more totalised feminist truth'.[36] Ien Ang goes on to point out that 'there are situations in which "women" as signifier for commonality would serve more to impede the self-presentation of particular groups of female persons ... than to enhance them'.[37]

It is widely understood that the primary (but not exclusive) site of struggle for Māori women is within a struggle for Māori independence. In my opinion, this necessarily includes the struggle for gender equality both within our culture and in the wider society. However, this struggle is being marginalised by anti-feminist sentiment, particularly within the wider movement for Tino Rangatiratanga. At a recent hui, a young man challenged the men present about how they were going to encourage equality for Māori women. One of the men responded, stating that it is all the fault of colonisation that Māori women are oppressed and suggested (of course) that a return to traditional gender relations would sort all that out. Indeed, this could be considered the depth of the debate/dialogue/discussion, in some quarters at least, around the issue of gender and the cultural positioning of Māori women at this time.

It is my hypothesis that a strident, vocal and distinct Māori 'feminist' voice is now distinctly absent within the independence movement. I believe the voices of feminist Māori women who led much of the protest movement through the seventies and eighties have been all but silenced or have gone underground. Many Māori women are fearful I believe, that naming Māori women's subordination will either be seen as, or actually be, anti-Māori and 'divisive to national unity'. As Kathie Irwin remembers of Māori activist groups in the early 1980s:

> the declared racism of the women's movement was thus a real deterrent for Māori women vaguely or even passionately interested in women's issues. The message was simple: women's issues are part of the Pākehā agenda; Pākehā have colonised this country and our minds; if you want to be included in Māori groups, then forget about women's issues.[38]

What, we might ask nearly twenty years on, has changed? It seems to me that since that time, the discourses around the reclamation of traditional gender roles may have actually become more entrenched and we are therefore continuing to see a Māori feminists' movement being co-opted/diverted/marginalised by the guilt-laden discourse of 'divisiveness'. But what are the ramifications for national unity if women's relative powerlessness is absent from the agenda? Margaret Jolly paraphrases Grace Mera Molisa's views on this:

> In the political process prior to independence, Molisa saw women as being without power. But she argued that this had to be changed in the process of attaining independence; it could not be delayed until afterwards. 'Otherwise our achievement of Independence will only be a half victory. A victory for the freedom of men but not women'.[39]

I am not suggesting that Māori women have not led and are not leaders; indeed, as Radhika Mohanram suggests (and we all know), Māori women have been central to the maintenance and transmission of Māori culture as well as participating in economic and political struggle.[40] However, if Māori women's emancipation is not central to the Māori struggle then as Mohanram articulates from Partha Chaterjee's article (which discusses India's struggle for independence) it may well be only a partial liberation. She says:

> it was necessary to mobilise women who constituted half the brown population. Yet the mobilisation for Indian emancipation did not necessarily include the emancipation of Indian women. They had to be reinscribed into a new form of patriarchy, one carrying the markers of colonialism and nationalism.[41]

In order to explore more fully whose interests are being served, I want to return briefly to Shohat's question: 'who is mobilising what in the articulation of the past, deploying what identities, identifications and representations, and in the name of what political vision and goals?'[42] Given that Māori women have been responsible at least in part for the construction of Māori women's identities which promote our status, our uniqueness and our mana (indeed the notion of 'mana wāhine' as a positive and affirming phrase I believe can be sourced within contemporary Māori women's discourse), it may be that Māori women ourselves have been articulating the past and deploying identities as a form of resistance in order that we will share more equally in a collective political vision. However, one must also ponder Shohat's question seriously in terms of how Māori women's discourses in turn have been informed by a distinctly Māori male hegemony, whose deployment may represent a political vision in which Māori women don't feature more than 'as a metaphor for the (independent) state and therefore become the scaffolding upon which men construct national identity'.[43]

While Mohanram believes that 'Māori men have constructed the Māori nation/female to reflect their own identity'[33] and that in 'no sphere do Māori women exercise autonomous agency; nowhere are they separate from Māori men or the Māori nation',[44] Māori women have been involved in constructing our own identities – yet these are always linked to Māori men and indeed to Māori society as a whole. This is part of an inclusive cultural ethos which we are trying to re/construct, one where we are linked interdependently in equality, this being the fundamental notion of community which espouses collective (and to a more limited degree individual) rights and responsibilities.

Māori men, as men, already have a distinct and entrenched advantage over Māori women and we must not assume they will relinquish or share this power readily. Indeed, as tribal leaders within the current settlement process, it is Māori men who are amassing a substantial power base. The economic development thrust over the past 15 years has also been led primarily by Māori men along capitalist, corporate lines, which is in direct contradiction with 'traditional' collective values. This could be seen as the selective deployment by Māori men of identities and discourses about authenticity and tradition in their own interests, but which are promoted as being in the interests of us all. As Ripeka Evans clearly points out, within the many organisations, trusts, incorporations and rūnanga

> the power and decision-making process of these organisations is in the hands of a small oligarchic menagerie of Māori men, businessmen, politicians, bureaucrats and lawyers, or otherwise more commonly known as the boy's club.

She goes on to state that

> There is no system guaranteeing a place for Māori women within our own institutions or within the new organisations which have evolved to manage our assets. Any talk of structural change sends some of our Māori men into a tail-spin about 'cultural correctness' and 'making waves'. There is a high powered selective amnesia about just what it takes to make change.[45]

In brief conclusion, I return and respond to Mohanram's statement regarding Māori women's agency, by asking this question: is it necessary within 'our' reconstructive process that Māori women do or continue to create/recreate spaces where we can exercise autonomous agency? Given the environment, I think it imperative. In terms of the Tino Rangatiratanga movement, perhaps the establishment of a more cohesive, coordinated and focused women's wing/arm/ network to theorise, to identify strategies for change, to research, develop and write, and to inform and challenge the wider movement and culture may be a starting point/continuation of Māori women's resistance and aspirations for equality within the struggle for Māori independence. It is self evident that those actively involved in this struggle (least of all the women) are not the power brokers in the Māori world, however I think it is imperative that a significant part of the movement's role is to act as the conscience (as well as the strategists) of our reconstruction. This will require some serious time to be spent in discussion and debate in order that the politics promoted reflect the necessary centrality of Māori women's liberation.

I am conscious that a focus on our past is essential, if not fundamental, to an understanding of our future. The ongoing project of reconstructing our communities must reflect the continuous *critical* engagement of 'traditional' values and practices with our changing cultural and political needs and aspirations.

Notes

1   K. Irwin, 'Toward Theories of Maori Feminisms' in Rosemary DuPlessis (ed.), *Feminist Voices: Women's Studies Text for Aotearoa/NZ* (Oxford University Press, Auckland, 1992), pp. 6-7.

2   The 'Fiscal Envelope' refers to the National Government proposal in 1994–5 to 'settle' all claims stemming from the Treaty of Waitangi 'fully and finally' by the year 2010, within a specified sum of money.

3   Irwin, p. 16.

4   Kauwhau notes for St Matthews in the City (unpublished sermon) 2 March 1997; J. Te Paa, Kauwhau notes for the Cathedral (unpublished sermon) 16 March 1997.

5   L. Mead (a.k.a. Tuhiwai Smith), 'Nga Aho o te Matauranga Maori: The Multiple Layers of Struggle by Maori in Education', PhD Thesis, Auckland University, 1996, pp. 2-3.

6   E. Shohat, cited in R. Mohanram, 'The Construction of Place: Maori Feminism and Nationalism in Aotearoa/New Zealand', *NWSA Journal*, 6 (1994), p. 54.

7   Trinh T. Minh-Ha 'Not You/Like You: Post Colonial Women and the Interlocking Questions of Identity and Difference', in Gloria Anzaldua, *Making Face, Making Soul/Haciendo Caras: Creative and Critical Perspectives by Feminists of Colour* (Aunt Lute Books, San Francisco, 1990), p. 371.

8   Ibid., p. 373.

9   Ibid., p. 375.

10 Ibid., p. 374.

11 E. Shohat, cited in R. Mohanram, p. 54.

12 P. Johnson & L. Pihama, 'The Marginalisation of Maori Women', in *Hecate: Special Aotearoa/New Zealand Issue*, 20:2 (1994), p. 90.

13 Linda Tuhiwai Smith, cited in Johnson & Pihama, p. 91.

14 Johnson & Pihama, p. 88.

15 A. Salmond, 'Te Ao Tawhito', Lecture, Auckland University, 1995.

16 Mead, p. 2.

17 Johnson & Pihama, p. 6.

18 Irwin, p. 7.

19 V. Kupenga, E. Rata, T. Nepi, 'Whaia te Iti Kahurangi: Maori Women Reclaiming Autonomy' in Witi Ihimaera (ed.), *Te Ao Marama 2, Regaining Aotearoa: Maori Writers Speak Out* (Reed Books, Auckland, 1993), p. 305.

20 Smith, cited in Johnson & Pihama, p. 90.

21 Taiamoni Tongamoa, 'Overview', in Tongamoa (ed.), *Pacific Women: Roles and Status of Women in Pacific Societies* (Institute of Pacific Studies, U.S.P. Suva, 1988), pp. 88-92.

22 Kate Millet, cited in A. Poananga, 'The Colonisation of Literature', in *Te Whakamarama – The Maori Law Bulletin*, Issue 10, Pipiri 1991.

23 Grace Mera Molisa, cited in M. Jolly, 'The Politics of Difference: Feminism, Colonialism and Decolonisation in Vanuatu', in Bottomley, Gillian, Marie de Lepervanche & Jeannie Martin (eds), *Intersexions: Gender, Class, Culture, Ethnicity.* (Allen and Unwin, Sydney, 1991), p. 58.

24 Waitangi Day (6 February) is the country's 'national day' to commemorate the signing of the Tiriti o Waitangi (Treaty of Waitangi) in 1840 between Māori and the British Crown. At the commemorations in 1997 the Leader of the Opposition, Helen Clark, was challenged by Māori politician John Delamere for sitting on the speaker's bench – a place he considered traditionally reserved for men.

25 Te Uira, Manihera, 'Learning and Tapu' in Michael King (ed.), *Te Ao Hurihuri:*

Aspects of Maoritanga (Reed Books, Auckland, 1992), p. 9.

26 *NZ Herald*, 8 February 1997.

27 S. Coney, *NZ Herald*, 16 February 1997.

28 Georgina Te Heuheu is a Māori woman politician. Helen Clark (a Pākehā woman), was Leader of the Opposition.

29 Irwin, op. cit., pp. 8-9.

30 R. Evans, 'The Negation of Powerlessness: Maori Feminism, a Perspective', *Hecate: Special Aotearoa/New Zealand*, 20:2 (1994), pp. 53-65

31 Ranginui Walker, *NZ Herald*, 11 February 1997.

32 M. Szaszy, 'Me Aro Koe ki te Ha o Hineahuone', in Witi Ihimaera (ed.), *Te Ao Marama 2, Regaining Aotearoa: Maori Writers Speak Out* (Reed Books, Auckland 1993), p. 289.

33 Ibid., p 290.

34 J. Carter, 'In and Around the Idea and Actuality of Maori Feminism' (unpublished paper), 1997.

35 Haunani Kay Trask, 'Pacific Island Women and White Feminism', in *From a Native Daughter: Colonialism and Sovereignty in Hawai'i* (Common Courage Press, Monroe, Maine, 1993), p. 265.

36 Ien Ang, 'I'm A Feminist But ... "Other" Women and Postnational Feminisms' in Rosemary Pringle and Barbara Caine (eds), *Transitions: New Australian Feminisms* (Allen & Unwin, Sydney, 1995), p. 64.

37 Ibid., p. 65.

38 K. Irwin, 'Maori Feminism' in Witi Ihimaera (ed.), *Te Ao Marama 2, Regaining Aotearoa: Maori Writers Speak Out* (Reed Books, Auckland, 1993), p. 301.

39 M. Jolly, 'The Politics of Difference: Feminism, Colonialism and Decolonisation in Vanuatu' in Gillian Bottomley, Marie de Lepervanche & Jeannie Martin (eds), *Intersexions: Gender, Class, Culture, Ethnicity* (Allen & Unwin, Sydney, 1991), p. 59.

40 R. Mohanram, 'The Construction of Place: Maori Feminism and Nationalism in Aotearoa/New Zealand', *NWSA Journal*, 6 (1994), p. 68.

41 Ibid.

42 E. Shohat, cited in Mohanram, p. 54.

43 Ibid.

44 Mohanram, p. 69.

45 R. Evans, 'Maori Women as Agents of Change', *Te Pua*, 3:1 (1994), p. 35.

THREE

Education in Western Samoa:
Reflections on my Experiences

LONISE TANIELU

This is the story of my formal educational experiences. My story is necessarily interspersed with digressions in my attempts at making my critical stand on certain issues clearer. It is a story which represents, in a lot of ways, the school experiences of many Samoans and quite possibily other peoples who 'owe' their formal education to the missionaries and colonisation. It also serves as an empirically-based analysis, which identifies and seeks to provide an understanding of the reasons why many school practices were and are not 'senseless' to us (and thus have been consolidated and have survived to the present), even though humanists, educators, psychologists, sociologists, anthropologists and modern missionaries point to them as senseless, socially demeaning, and psychologically and educationally deadly.

I was born in 1948 in the village of Solosolo (about 24 kilometres east of Apia, the capital of Samoa), where my father was the faifeau (minister) for the Congregational Christian Church of Samoa (formerly the London Missionary Society [LMS] Church), in that village. I am the third child in a family of four boys and two girls.

I started my formal education when I was three years old in the Vasega Faitau Pi, at the aoga faifeau, (also known as the aoga Samoa), learning how to read the Pi Tautau, recite tauloto and answer fesili o le Tusi Paia. I was in the Vasega Faitau Pi until I was five years old, then I was promoted to the Vasega Muamua. These formative years were to shape my lasting impressions of what formal education is about: sitting still, keeping quiet, listening carefully, speaking only when asked, being rewarded with the stroke of the stick or broom for misbehaviour.

My first year in the Vasega Faitau Pi introduced me to my first exam and the world of school competition in the suega faifeau. These exams were held in the August school holidays and everyone involved looked forward to them, parents and children alike. A fortnight before the exam day, the older pupils (Vasega Fa I le Vasega Ono), slept at the faifeau's house to study late into the night and wake up early for more exam cramming. The coveted prize for the dux (sili o le Vasega Ono), the big Samoan bible and hymn book, was sought after by each village in our five village church district. It was a most highly competitive undertaking. It was a competition not only for the exam candidates but for the villages, parents and faifeau also. Each village had a turn at hosting these exams. It did not matter if we had to wake up at three in the morning for the long walk, if it was the farthest village from ours that was hosting the exams. It was worth it because our village, one of the biggest in the district, was sure to snatch a few sili.

In the Vasega Faitau Pi exam, we had to read the Pi Tautau, recite our tauloto and answer fesili o le Tusi Paia, without making any mistakes to gain full marks. There was a lot of excitement and joy for those children who performed well, but there was also much unhappiness and crying as the preschoolers who forgot their tauloto or refused to read the Pi Tautau were threatened with physical and verbal abuses of all sorts: E le fafaga oe (You won't be fed), Faatali oe pe a oo I le fale (You wait until we get home), Nao lou ma I lenei tamaititi matua valea tele (This stupid child puts me to shame), and so on.

Some children got hidings there and then, and the more a child cried, the more the abuse, to hopefully silence him/her. But the child who was hurt and frustrated, and did not understand why s/he was undergoing such treatment, naturally reacted by crying more and louder, so the palm of the hand over the mouth muffled the child's screams. Because these exams were so dreadfully competitive, it did not occur to the parents, the mothers especially, who were more concerned that their children did well, that the children were under a lot of unnecessary pressure, being in strange surroundings amongst unfamiliar faces. A child that was continuously exposed to such treatment would either mentally swim or sink, and some that sank drowned, never to swim again. These experiences either make or break the intellectual development and growth of children. This historical pattern has been transmitted to the present where I am experiencing it today, with the mothers and their children, in the church parish where my husband is the minister, and I am the coordinator and supervisor of the aoga amata (Samoan language nest), the Sunday School and the women's fellowship group.

In 1994, I carried out an action research project as part of my Masters programme, on the practice of physical and verbal abuse in our aoga amata. I identified this as a serious and most disruptive practice. The practice was considered unconducive to the qualitative physical, emotional, social and intellectual development of the children. It was most upsetting for the abused children, unsettling for the other preschoolers and frustrating for me as supervisor of the nest. My efforts at convincing the abusing mothers that there were other and better ways of disciplining children were often thwarted by the mothers' own convictions and intrinsic beliefs in the infliction of pain as the only way of drumming sense into a child – Faamaini le pau ona uma lea o le faalogogata

(Sting the skin to stop misbehaviour). My relatively soft way of gentle but firm persuasion, talking to the child, guiding and facilitating his/her learning, 'would only spoil them', they said. Old habits die hard. These mothers were victims of such disciplinary measures in previous generations, as I was. The parents' general acceptance of corporal punishment as an essential child-rearing practice is largely influenced by their almost fanatical belief in biblical phrases such as 'o le sasa e tatau I le tua o le vale' (stupid people deserve a beating). (Proverbs 10, verse 13).

My project turned into an educational experience, with some measure of success for us at the nest, after sessions of teaching child development and psychology, and the school nurse's demonstrations showed how children's hearing is affected by excessive noise and slapping on the ears. At least now, during the nest sessions, the mothers leave the children alone. I hate though to think of what might be happening in the home.

The pedagogical practices of the aoga tulaga lua (primary school), also known as the aoga palagi, closely resembled those of the aoga faifeau. A double dosage of these in the schools, plus a third dose at home, meant that many students went through their schooling as docile objects, learning very little, controlled by the fear of a hiding if they made mistakes. Rebellious behaviour was a relatively rare occurrence due to the high prevalence of these suppressive practices. There were students who were almost always last in our exams, as if they were destined to be in that position. They often bore the brunt of the teacher's wrath, which was mostly directed at those who were branded valea.

The results (places and marks) of all who sat in both these schools' exams were read out – and still are – during their respective annual prize-givings. These were special occasions when the villagers congregated to praise and admonish children and to compare their placings and performances. The students, as much as their parents and relatives, were in this competition together. Parents encouraged their respective children to do well and to vie for the top places, because the holders of these were seen as superior and more intelligent than the bottom students.

Knowledge was considered a possession that distinguished the superior from the inferior. Because I was socialised this way also, I harboured definite notions about illiterate people as less knowledgeable, backward, simple and ignorant, fit only for labour and domestic chores; they were to be controlled and manipulated by literate people. My beliefs were the results of my schooling which had the function of indoctrinating us into believing that the print literacy opened doors to better things and a better life, an 'unSamoan' life.

This competitive goal structure in the schools, plus the constant encouragement of students to out-perform their peers, has had a strong socialising effect on the Samoan people. Children who performed well were praised and encouraged and were showered with much alofa. Often the parents whose children continuously performed poorly in the exams became discouraged and eventually accepted 'dumbness' as the fate of their children. Consequently, some parents stopped their children from going to school altogether saying, 'E leai sau mea o maua mai le aoga, e sili pe a e nofo e fai feau I le fale' (You are not learning anything at school, much better if you stay home to do the chores).

The tendency for children to compete in school often interfered with their capacity to adapt when cooperation was needed to solve academic problems. Firstly, the children lacked the experience to work cooperatively, even though they achieved goals this way before they started school. Secondly, a student who could work out the problem often feigned ignorance or refused to share his/her knowledge with peers, in case another student became more knowledgeable. Teachers encouraged these practices, either consciously or unconsciously, through their expectations of the students and their tendency to focus their attention on the bright students. Because teachers were also under great pressure to teach to an exam syllabus, slow students became neglected. Cooperative learning was then confined to entertainment, feasting and cleaning purposes, learning dances and items, preparing food and beautifying the school for special occasions.

The term 'formal' lived up to its name in describing my education, both in and out of school. My home upbringing as a faifeau's daughter was the epitome of formality itself. From a very early age, I was conditioned to sit quietly in the presence of older people, lower myself when walking in front of people, behave and address people appropriately, eat and drink sitting down and demonstrate modesty in whatever I did.[2] Modest behaviour included laughing softly, covering over the knees when sitting down, not visiting other people's homes or befriending boys, and especially keeping away from gossip-mongers. Much of the content of this education was influenced by the earlier teaching of 'civilised' behaviour by the missionaries, such as covering up as much of the girl's body as possible, and other Victorian dress codes.

The faifeau's children were also expected to perform well in both the aoga faifeau and the aoga palagi. I learned to accept this as my fate and behaved accordingly, knowing no other way, but much of the time I lived a 'grin and bear it' existence. This civilised and mechanically acquired behaviour was to hinder to a large extent my own academic education, as I soon found out when I went to school in Apia. My village-grown and relatively sheltered lifestyle posed limits to my participation in classroom activities. Because I was not encouraged to speak out of turn, I stuck to my quiet way of learning without querying much.

On the other hand, the faifeau's children were the most privileged children in the village. We lived well, ate well, dressed well and learned well. Because the faifeau was an educated person, his children had relatively more chance of getting far in school. Even though there was much suppression of freedom to express ourselves (orally especially), we threw ourselves into our studies encouraged not only in the school but in the home. Our father helped us with homework and made sure that we did it, as well as encouraging us to read both in Samoan and in English. There were not many books in our home, but the few we had were better than nothing and we read them to the point of memorisation. In the village, this help was not readily available in most homes. The faifeau and his children formed part of the elite and privileged few in Samoan society and still do. But the faifeau helped a lot also in the education of the village children. His teachings were not confined to biblical knowledge. During our aoga po for example, he taught the children general knowledge and arithmetic.The aoga faifeau syllabus also included some geography and science.

I entered Solosolo Village Primary School when I was six years old. Throughout my primary school years (1955-1960), from Primer One to Standard Four, I had two lots of exams to contend with every year. One for the aoga Samoa and one for the aoga palagi. This was standard for all village children. My school day started at eight in the morning until one in the afternoon, with the aoga palagi. The aoga Samoa started at three and finished at five in the evening. From seven to eight at night, we had aoga faitau Tusi Paia. This was the pattern for most days during the week. Most of the time in these schools was spent listening to the teacher, rote learning information, reciting, writing in our books or copying work off the board. So much was taught yet so little was learned. If the parents had any complaints, about the aoga faifeau especially, they were unheard, as it was generally believed that the more education their children had the better for them. Many claimed they owed a lot of their own educational success and wisdom to the aoga faifeau. Some only had an aoga faifeau education.

Most of our primary school teachers had only a primary school education (intermediate and secondary schooling having only been introduced in the 1950s), though they had been through teacher training. Most of the teaching and learning was done in Samoan, even for the English language classes, despite the fact that exams in the standard classes were all in English, except for Samoan.

Despite the restrictions and rigidities of my education during these years, they were some of the most memorable times in my life and I continually reminisce about those good times. Life during these years was not all mechanical and routine. There were opportunities for us as children to think and act independently and creatively, especially outside the classrooms. We played a lot with what the local physical environment offered. We made and play-acted with our pepe fune, polished mapu fetau for the marble-shooting tournaments and made balloons from the pulu tree leaf buds. We swam like dolphins in the sea and, in between swimming, we made sandcastles and teased the waves.

Other favourite pastimes were racing our pulu boats on the sea water, making toy cars from lapalapa (coconut leaf stalks) and sneaking from home at night to watch entertainment at the village malae. Before we went to sleep, we always looked forward to listening to fagogo and tagigafagogo. There was much socialising during those years amongst the village children. The aoga faifeau was often an excuse to get away from the numerous home chores and the children were in no hurry to get home after the afternoon aoga. Some planned it so they had just enough time to shower and get ready for the aoga po at the faifeau's house.

Story telling is an old Samoan art. It was part of our oral literacy and traditional education. Bedtime stories are not new to the Samoans. Grandparents played a vital role in the education of their grandchildren as they were the story tellers. This story telling served very significant purposes, some of which include the following: the handing down of cultural, historical and moral values; the acquisition of cognitive skills of comprehension, listening and critical thinking, numeracy skills, concepts of height, depth and volume; geography skills about the spatial distribution of fauna and flora. The telling and chanting of the fagogo provided opportunities for music and drama. Every so often, the story teller would pause to ask questions to test the children's understanding and the children were to say aue every now and then to show they were paying attention. Story telling was a great equaliser also. It served as a levelling device when the old and the young alike shared experiences without paying heed as to who ought to speak first or have the last say. It was an informal time in which the children were not expected to sit up straight or keep still. We could lie down and we could ask questions. Caution to formality was relaxed and, after a hard day's work, we were lulled to sleep by the chanting of the fagogo. The art and the process of story telling are now practically lost. A more mobile and modern lifestyle has done away with this necessary element of the Samoan child's education.

When we entered the classroom, it was a different set-up altogether. Half the time we were reprimanded or caned for talking or not finishing assigned work. We were either comparing our marbles or discussing swimming after aoga faifeau. These diversions provided relief from the monotony of the military-like exercises in the classroom. In the aoga faifeau, where we did not have desks, these diversions eased the back-breaking practice and discomfort of bending forward while writing on our slates, which we did most of the time. The long stick, strap and broom were necessary tools of the teacher's trade in those days and no one questioned their frequent use. Classroom learning was an apprenticeship in passivity and an exercise in social control. The measure of a good teacher was a quiet, disciplined and obedient class and neatly-kept books. It did not matter whether the work in the books was correct as long as it was neatly presented.

At the end of my standard four year (1959), there was a national exam to select students for the aoga itumalo (district intermediate school). The Anoamaa (name of our district) District School was only opened three years before and was only taking in a limited number of students because of the shortage of classrooms and qualified teachers. Six of us from Solosolo Primary were selected while most other schools from our twelve village district had three or four. The district school had three levels, Form One E, Form One A and Form Two. Form One E was the new entrants class. There was an exam at the end of our Form One E year (1960) to select students for Form One A at Samoa College, which then had a primary division. We were given an intelligence test in which we had to match symbols and did problems that tested our comprehension. Much of the content of the test was unfamiliar and I guessed a lot. I must have guessed well as I was one of three students that got selected from our school for Samoa College. The rest of our class proceeded to Form One A at the district school.

Samoa College was a far cry from the village and district schools. It was for most of us a 'culture shock' experience. There were many 'firsts' for us that year. Our principal was a palagi man, we had palagi children in our class and we had our own desks. At the village and district schools, we were crammed five pupils to one long desk. At Samoa College we were not allowed to speak Samoan and the punishment for speaking our own language was weeding grass for two hours in the hot sun. Samoa College had strict rules about lateness and truancy. We had to stand to attention every morning after the raising of the Union Jack, while the principal hollered at us to come early to school, wear the proper uniform, speak English at all times and not to loiter in the corridors. If the village and district schools were formal, they were nothing compared to Samoa College. For me and no doubt for other rural students too, having to adapt to a new school as well as to an urban lifestyle, was alienating. I had to stay with an aunty in Apia because of the irregular bus service from our village. Any confidence that I had, and the novelty of attending the top school in the country, soon wore off.

Although our teacher was a gentle lady who encouraged us to do well, to participate in class and group activities and to ask questions if we did not understand, I was reluctant to speak English and only spoke when asked. The fear of getting put on detention for speaking Samoan overcame any desire to ask questions. My self-esteem was at a low ebb. My past informal and formal education taught me not to query anything. My days were then mostly spent listening to the teacher and doing book work. In the absence of any verbal participation in class and group activities, I perfected my listening skills. I did not like this relatively new way of learning where we were encouraged to think independently, be creative, express our thoughts, work independently in doing problems and think far ahead. I liked it better when we rote learned times-tables, poems and notes and recited them in class, copied work off the board and called out answers in unison. I was good at arithmetic but the new maths, where we had to solve equations, was out of my league. The transition from the village and district schools to Samoa College left a learning gap that needed bridging. I lacked the semantic resources and essential schemata to close this gap. I missed my family, I missed the village children, I missed the rural life where I knew exactly what I had to do and where I was going. I preferred copying notes into my book to getting up in front of the class to read an English essay or doing morning news in English.

Our end of year exam 'failed' some students who had to go back to their respective district schools. There was no logic behind failing those students. They should have been given chances to settle down to a new school, let alone a strange urban lifestyle. The stigma of failing from Samoa College was much more severe than failing from the village or district schools. It was generally believed that the only reason a student failed from Samoa College was because s/he was valea (dumb), and the valea child was the luma o le aiga (shame of the family). Samoa College was so selective in the type of students it retained that it failed to consider the psychological and social consequences of such practices. Its reputation as the top school in the country had to be maintained at all costs and only the tamaititi poto went to Samoa College.

The selection process for entrance to the primary division at Samoa College and later to the Leififi Intermediate School from the district school, was very strict and confining. It was based on mental ability, age and size. Big and tall twelve year olds were often not selected because their sizes did not equate with the idea of the normal size of a twelve year old. Even with birth certificates as proof, the examiners often did not believe that some of these students were telling the truth about their ages. My own younger brother and sister suffered such fates for being too big and too tall for their ages. Each candidate was screened before the test. Whatever the reason, the inclusion of size and age could hardly be justified as rational policy as often in those days, children did not start school until they were much older than the official entry age of six. It was most unfair for some very bright students who missed out because of their sizes and ages. It was also an elitist process that chose only two or three students from each district school, from an average class of forty students.

The year 1961 was the last year of the primary level at Samoa College. Our class left Samoa College to merge with the Malifa Primary Form Two classes, to start what is now the Leififi Intermediate School. We were the pioneer students of that school in 1962, the year Western Samoa became independent.

The year 1962 proved to be yet another unsettling year for me. Getting to know the Malifa students was quite something. They were more outgoing, more expressive, and being urban-reared, referred to us as o le au mea kua peki (them things from the back, country bumpkins from the wop wops), insinuating that they were more civilised than us rural kids. Their progress to Form Two was easy compared to ours and they outnumbered us three to one. They were familiar with the school surroundings and teachers and they had had more contact with palagi teachers and students. They spoke English more fluently and their primary schooling was in a relatively more adequately resourced educational environment.

Malifa then was an elitist school as it always had been since the Germans set it up in the early 1900s. It was far better resourced than the village and district schools. The Malifa students have always accounted for over half of Samoa College's Form Three intake. With the upgrading of all district schools to Junior Secondary level (Form Three to Form Five), by 1973 Form One and Form Two classes were added on to all village primary schools in the country. In theory, this gave every Form Two student throughout Samoa an equal chance of getting into Samoa College, yet the Leififi students have continued to out-perform their rural peers.

Complete equality of provision can never be achieved in a system that depends on the willingness of parents and community to find resources to supplement those provided by the government. Schools in better off communities, like the Malifa and Leififi schools, will always have higher levels of equipment and resources. The rural parents that flock to Malifa to acquire places for their children cannot be blamed for wanting the best education for their children. Even children who do not speak English at home are being enrolled for places in the English-speaking classes because their parents believe this is the key to better education.

At Leififi Intermediate, we had the same principal from Samoa College, but most of the teachers were former Malifa teachers. I had a palagi woman as a teacher for the first time. At the end of the year, we sat the Form Two national exam and over half of our Form Two students were selected for Samoa College. I went back to Samoa College as a third former in 1963. In the four years from 1960 to 1963, I went through four changes of schools and three external exams. At Samoa College, I continued in my passive way of learning from Form Three to Form Six. I had two years in Form Five, one year in Lower Five and another in Upper Five. The idea was to strengthen our background knowledge, of English in particular, in preparation for the New Zealand School Certificate Exam at the end of our Upper Five year. In our sixth form year (1967), we sat the New Zealand University Entrance Exam and in the same year applied for scholarships to go overseas for further studies. Out of about seventy applications from our school, seventeen received scholarships. I wanted to apply for a nursing scholarship but our principal suggested that I apply for a more academic scholarship so I opted for primary teaching and received a scholarship to study at Palmerston North Teachers College. I graduated from there in 1969 and in 1970 taught at Russell Primary School in Porirua before I went back to teach in Samoa in 1971.

What I learned about child-centred education at teachers' college, and practised during my teaching in New Zealand, was soon put aside as I carried on the tradition of teaching bodies of knowledge, to an exam-oriented syllabus, as a Social Science teacher. I taught at the Form Two level for a year at my old school, Leififi Intermediate. For the five years after that I taught at junior secondary level, teaching English and Social Science to Form Four and Form Five students.

In 1977, I received a scholarship to study towards a Bachelor of Education degree at the University of the South Pacific in Suva, Fiji. I was married then to a church minister and had three daughters whom I left behind with my husband while I went away to study. The decision to leave behind a six month old baby was a most difficult one to make. The odds were against me in making this decision. Most people were against my taking up the scholarship. The usual 'logical' explanations, that the mother's first priority was her children and husband, the baby was too young to be without its mother, it is not right for a minister's wife to go off like that on her own and so on, made me more determined that I was not going to pass up the opportunity to further my education. I was responsible for my own choice and I had the ability and power to choose my response even against all odds. My behaviour was a product of my own conscious choice. I was driven by a value-laden desire to make progress in my education, to improve my teaching career which, in the end, would benefit not only me and my family but many others. As a woman, I had respect for myself and believed that I could do better and go further; and no one was going to take that self-respect away unless I let them. My determination paid off, supported wholeheartedly by my husband and my parents, who were prepared to do their best for my children and stood by me and my decision.

At the University, I majored in education and geography. My curriculum studies struck a different chord in the education song that I had been singing in my years of teaching in Samoa. They encouraged me to think seriously about the questions: 'Education for What?' and 'What is Relevant Education?' In response to the essay topic: *In what ways do you consider the present curriculum of secondary schools in your part of the South Pacific relevant, and what in ways is it not?* I wrote, 'The present curriculum of the secondary schools in Western Samoa is exam-oriented. It is geared towards passing New Zealand School Certificate and University Entrance. In the application, the practicality and the depth of the imparted knowledge lies the irrelevance of the present curriculum...' I was encouraged by my lecturers to polish up this essay for publication but I did not want to be seen as a 'radical' then. At least that was what I thought at the time. I guess my upbringing got the better of me. I graduated in 1978.

Our family moved to Suva in 1979 where my husband had a teaching job at the Pacific Theological College. I stayed on and taught at the university as a foundation Social Science lecturer and geography tutor. In 1981, we moved to New Zealand when my husband was called to the Porirua parish in Wellington. In 1988, we moved back to Samoa for my husband's appointment as general secretary of our church.

Our move back to Samoa gave me the chance to serve my bond with the government for the years of study in Suva. This service had been put on hold as my husband's work kept us away from Samoa. I taught full time at the Secondary Teachers College and part time at the National University of Samoa (NUS). In 1991, I was appointed assistant director for the Examination and Curriculum Development Unit (ECDU) in the Education Department. As head of the unit, I pushed for a strong internal assessment component to be part of every Western Samoa School Certificate (WSSC) and Pacific Senior School Certificate (PSSC) subject. I envisaged a fair weighting between the exam and the internal assessment component so that students would not be disadvantaged unnecessarily by the over reliance on the examination as the sole determinant of their performance, especially at the senior secondary level. It did not surprise me that the general feeling among the secondary school teachers then was not in favour of such a move. They implied that there was no 'infrastructure' in place for such a policy, but more perhaps the problem was the teachers' own internalised belief in the exam as the most objective and fairest form of assessment. The South Pacific Board of Examinations and Assessment (SPBEA) had offered to help out and had already produced a comprehensive plan to be trialled for internal assessment in the PSSC English. It was not that the teachers were unaware of the advantages of internal assessment, but rather that the culture of teaching in Samoa is dominated by norms of fitting into established structures and routines. Any educational innovation, even one considered of value, can be very hard to put through the system. We left Samoa at the end of 1992 for yet another call to a parish in New Zealand, this time in Auckland.

I am basically a social science teacher with mostly a physical geography background. My teacher training and university studies provided some background in education. The inadequacies I felt about having to teach anthropology at NUS for three years without an anthropology background, working as an administrator and policy maker in the Education Department without any administration training, plus my own need to keep in tune with current educational developments, were to prompt me, when our family moved back to New Zealand, to study towards a Masters degree in educational administration at Auckland University. The courses that I took in 1994 and 1995 have been of great relevance and most inspiring. They have not only broadened the educational perspectives of a physical geographer but have engendered within me a compelling urge to write. They have rekindled a waning sense of obligation to an education system that I am part and parcel of. I write now hopefully to contribute towards a better understanding of some of the problems of Samoa's education system. I am a product of that system, having been a student, a teacher, a teacher educator, administrator and policy maker in it.

Notes

1 Every Samoan child is expected to know the *gagana faaaloalo* (language of respect) and the *gagana o aso uma* (everyday language). The use of each depends on the status of the person one is addressing. For example, when asking someone, 'Where are you going?', one says to a paramount chief or his wife, '*A afio I fea?*'; to a talking chief (orator), '*A sosopo I fea?*'; to the orator's wife, '*A maliu I fea?*'; to the *faifeau* or his wife, '*A susu I fea?*'; to an untitled person, '*A agai I fea*?'; to one's peers and family, '*A e alu I fea?*'

4 L.S. Tanielu, 'Ideological Shifts in Western Samoan Education: A Critical Analysis,' M Ed. Dissertation, Auckland University, 1995.

FOUR

Learning Sexuality:
Young Samoan Women

ANNEMARIE TUPUOLA

The Dilemma

She cried bitterly in frustration
cast into the world of the unwanted
the young mother-to-be
was faced with a bitter decision ...
... the solution lay within her ...
She had marred her family picture
the pride which had been for so long upheld
was now in fragments
scattered across the evening sky. [1]

Introductory Thoughts – A Personal Reflection

In recent years Pacific Islands communities and health authorities in New Zealand have become concerned with the growing number of 'unintended pregnancies' and abortions among Pacific Island women. According to 1993 statistics, approximately three quarters of hospitalisations of Pacific Island women aged between fifteen and twenty-five years were for pregnancy, childbirth and health services related to reproduction.[2] Between 1990 and 1992 the estimated abortion rate for Pacific Islands women was 1,020 per 1,000 women compared to 376 per 1,000 for non-Pacific Islands women.[3]

In my opinion these figures should alert us to some of the cultural dilemmas and communication barriers faced by young Pacific Islands women in New Zealand. I applaud current services such as Awhitia, Family Planning Clinics and the Pacific Islands AIDS Trust, which aim to educate Pacific Islands women about sexuality, contraceptives and safe sex and which involve the participation of Pacific Islands people. However, I have a major concern about the effectiveness of the context and procedures taken by both the Pacific Islands communities and health educators to educate young Pacific women about sexuality.

I attend various Pacific Islands and Samoan Health community fonos (forums) to seek more information on how these communities view youth health, especially sex education. These gatherings tend to reinforce the authoritative and hierarchical social structure of fa'aSamoa (Samoan culture) and are in many instances disempowering for subordinate members – the youth and young women.[4] In general, there is an unspoken expectation at these meetings for youth, in particular young women, to listen and defer to the perspectives and decisions of those in authority – the older and elite members of the communities. Occasionally similar power relationships prevail (perhaps at an unconscious level) in some sexuality programmes designed and implemented by Pacific Islands elders. Although it is encouraging that elders are taking the initiative in the area of sex education, the effectiveness of this must be questioned.

I have found through personal communication with young Samoan women that many are hesitant about discussing taboo subjects in the presence of adults, particularly as they see it violating Samoan principles of fa'aaloalo (respect) and ava (reverence). Another factor is confidentiality. Many fear the loss of privacy, especially as many of the educators are renowned members of their church, ethnic communities and neighbourhoods, possible relatives and family friends. In examining contemporary sexuality services it is crucial to acknowledge the differential power relations between Samoan youth and elders in New Zealand and to accept that the current expectation for young Samoan women to speak in the presence of adults or to publicly discuss matters of sexuality with ease is unrealistic.

The points of discussion in this article originate from my research for a Master of Arts thesis at Victoria University entitled, 'Critical Analysis of Adolescent Development – a Samoan Women's Perspective'. This research aimed to re-examine adolescent development theories within a Samoan context. Do Samoans, Samoan girls in particular, experience adolescence as defined by western psychologists, anthropologists and human developmentalists?[5] Many of the young women I interviewed as part of this research were critical of theories that posited adolescence as a stage where girls grow away from their families, have boyfriends and become individuals.[6] Their conflicted and strongly-held views about their own sexuality led me to focus on this aspect of the women's experience.

Here I will briefly discuss the Samoan principles of fa'aaloalo and ava (respect and obligation) to illustrate the rigid codes of conduct between elder/ aiga/male and the young woman. My simple synopsis here is not to underrate the compelling nature and influence of fa'aSamoa but rather to set the scene to show why learning sexuality may be a cultural dilemma for young Samoan women. In view of the heterogeneity of young Samoan women I introduce my research participants and their definitions of fa'aSamoa and sexuality. To capture the ease, comfort and open dialogue typical of my research I discuss aspects of my methodology that proved effective. Following that I include the painful and secretive experiences of these women to illustrate the contradictory principles and attitudes held by some Samoans toward female sexuality. The concluding section re-emphasises the cultural dilemmas and challenges faced by young Samoan women in New Zealand and suggests ways they can be effectively addressed in future sexuality and sex education programmes and services.

Realities of Fa'aSamoa Principles

Fa'aaloalo and ava are central to understanding traditional fa'aSamoa principles concerning young Samoan women and sexuality. To address these effectively I will begin by discussing the cultural dilemma I face as the author of this article. Is my objective to paint a picturesque view of fa'aSamoa or to expose the covert hypocrisies of Samoan culture with the associated risks of confirming the stereotyped views of the 'other' and of losing the future respect of Samoan people?[7] Writing this article is itself a cultural violation; within the social norms of traditional fa'aSamoa I, as a young Samoan woman, have no acquired right and privilege to speak of and about the Samoan culture. Culturally specific intricacies associated with public speech mean that many Pacific Islanders do not believe in the right for any Pacific Island person to speak for and about Pacific Islanders.[8] In accordance with traditional fa'aSamoa principles, the rightful speaker and author here should be an older Samoan woman.

The topic of this article has me in a further predicament. In discussing female sexuality I take numerous risks, particularly as Samoans are generally conservative in matters of sex and very protective of their private lives.[9] Such risks include losing any future status in my Samoan community and blemishing the honour of my family and ancestors. Through personal experience I am reminded of the severe and, at times, relentless unspoken disciplinary mechanisms of traditional fa'aSamoa and the intense fear of the possibility of ostracism from my aiga.

The aiga (extended family) plays a pivotal role in the lives of young Samoan women. Research by Samoan people provides differing views of the aiga. According to Taule'ale'ausumai, the aiga is the epitome of the collective and corporate nature of fa'aSamoa. Family life, she states, 'extends out beyond nuclear family incorporating uncles, aunties, both sets of grandparents and many cousins'.[10] The aiga maintain a central disciplinary role. They discipline the child to respectfully comply with the instructions of older relatives. To escape the severe punishments of the aiga, Samoan children learn to conceal their true feelings and soon become 'adept at … an outward demeanor pleasing to those in authority'.[11] Another primary function of the Samoa aiga (male relatives in particular) is to protect and control the sexuality of the unmarried Samoan girl:

> As sisters, their reproductive sexuality controlled (by their fathers and brothers), women symbolize the pinnacle of aganu'u or culture. A calculus of control over female sexuality suggests for female status a set of important transformations between nature and culture. As 'girls', they are virgins, sisters but not wives. To remain a virgin under the pressure to lose control is not understood as self-control, but rather as the control exerted by brothers over their sisters.[12]

In a highly structured and hierarchical society such as Samoa, female virgins are highly valued and cherished.[13] Unmarried women are held responsible for the status of their aiga and village and are therefore strictly watched and guarded from the time of their first menstruation.[14] Unlike her male peers, a girl finds it is no longer her wishes but those of 'her village and aiga that count'.[15] In honour of the feagaiga relationship the male relatives exert severe measures of control on the girl's sexuality to prevent the tarnishing of their family honour.[16] In other words, whatever her rank, her brothers exercise an active surveillance over her to ensure that she has little (if any) contact with male peers without their consent and knowledge. Failure to fulfil these expectations will mean that the girl is 'liable to [be punished] with great ferocity'.[17] Should the girl fall pregnant or should it be discovered that she is not a virgin the implications are enormous. Shore explains that:

> the implications ... are a total lack of control over a girl's sexuality by her brothers, and the complete triumph of personal desire. In cases like these, the usual norms that the brothers must respect and avoid close contact with their sisters are reversed, and the girls are subject to violent beatings at the hands of their brothers.[18]

Samoan women who obey the virtue of chastity before marriage are upheld as a source of pride for the aiga. Social positions accorded the highest cultural value for women are those in which 'sexuality remains controlled not by simple denial, but by elaborate arranged marriages'.[19] In many traditional Samoan societies, arranged marriages are held in the highest regard and in general offer the best cultural and economical prospects for the girl. Such arranged marriages are marked not only by 'careful negotiation and elaborate exchanges of toga ... fine mats ... food and implements of practical value' but also the triumph of the girl's aiga and male relatives.[20]

Among the fundamental principles of fa'aSamoa the expectation for young Samoan women to adhere to particular 'codes of honour' cannot be ignored.[21] Young Samoan women, as subordinate members of the social structure of Samoa, are forbidden to speak in the presence of adults, and elders in particular, on topics relating to the human body and sexuality. There are several reasons for the cocoon-like lifestyle of the young Samoan woman.[22] The aiga is a major control agent in her life. Its primary function is not only to protect the young woman but also to discipline her when she violates fundamental socio-cultural expectations. Young women who disobey face severe consequences. As often shown in literature on Samoan people women are beaten, labelled 'pa'umutu' ('prostitute'), ostracised from the aiga or alienated and isolated from their Samoan communities.[23] To escape these forms of punishment, some young women take drastic measures: some become pregnant deliberately to dishonour their families; some completely alienate themselves from their aiga and the culture; some even commit suicide.[24] The aiga's stringent codes of behaviour and the intense nature of discipline within traditional Samoan contexts may explain women's reluctance to openly discuss sexuality or to disobey the demands and decisions of their elders, aiga and male relatives.

Contemporary Views of Fa'aSamoa and Female Sexuality

The following discussion provides a critical and contemporary perception of traditional fa'aSamoa and its impact on female sexuality. I need to point out that although there are many positive aspects of fa'aSamoa, this particular account of my research highlights traumatic, complex and 'hidden' experiences of some young women – aspects of their experiences of sexuality which they feel have been kept silent for too long. The thirteen Samoan women in my research were aged between sixteen and twenty-nine years old. Seven were born and raised in New Zealand. Six were born in Samoa – of these, four are recent immigrants to New Zealand. Seven of the thirteen women had studied human development and ethnographic research at university.

The women were invited to participate through a 'snowball' sampling technique. I originally discussed my research with two young Samoan women and asked them to 'spread the word'. In turn, women interested in participating contacted me. Interestingly, although I was based in Wellington, word quickly spread as far afield as Auckland, so participants (myself included) came from diverse socio-economic, cultural and educational backgrounds in both cities. Four were tertiary students, two clerical workers, two sales and marketing assistants, three domestic executives and two were unemployed.

In acknowledgement of both the rural Samoa and urban New Zealand socio-cultural backgrounds of my participants it was necessary to incorporate into the research activities traditional fa'aSamoa principles alongside those of the palagi (European/Western) world.[25] In other words, while fa'aaloalo and ava were emphasised it was within a different context. My research required that all women respect each other's experiences and perspectives. It did not mean that younger women should defer and obey the views and requests of myself or older participants. Alongside the principles of respect and reverence were those common to the western world such as analysis, critique and verbal articulation. With the combination of these two cultural structures women were free to disagree with me and other participants, to display anger, pain, fear and to express these emotions in the knowledge that they would not be ostracised, and with the relief that other participants shared similar experiences.

Confidentiality and privacy became major issues. Women were reassured of their privacy by individual meetings, by writing their experiences down anonymously and by choosing the women they felt comfortable with in their group sessions. Each woman was also assigned a pseudonym to protect her from being recognised in the final text. Through a flexible methodology participants were able to shape the research and to analyse its process during all phases.[26] As seen in the following written comments made anonymously at the final session, this process was empowering and therapeutic for many of the women:

> This research helped me a lot. It gave me an inspiration of strength and inner peace. I felt very safe talking about my sexual experiences ... even though it was hard I felt I could trust the other women and the researcher. It was good that she was a Samoan researcher, it made a big difference – we had a common ground and that helped. I feel this research is so important. It is not very often that young Samoan girls get the opportunity to talk about their experiences. In the past, this has always been by our Samoan elders, the palagi intellects or those who are so far removed from our realities.

> I think this thesis made me take a good look at myself – it was a really empowering experience. I thought AnneMarie went out of her way to make me and the other women feel safe and comfortable. I was really surprised by the support I received from the women in this research ... I think I was a little reluctant to talk about sex at first, I didn't want our ideas to be labelled feminist or radical ... but it was neat how we could look at the text ... to make sure our ideas weren't misinterpreted [in the final research]. I feel privileged participating in this research ... it was well prepared and sensitive to my and other women's needs.

What were some of the women's views of fa'aSamoa values and protocol? Many participants critiqued the androcentric and ethnocentric principles of fa'aSamoa and attitudes of some elders toward young Samoan women. In their view fa'aSamoa epitomised moral contradictions, old fashioned expectations and gender-biased philosophies. Recent research on New Zealand-born Samoans emphasises similar issues and, like my participants, suggests a need for traditional fa'aSamoa customs to acknowledge modernity and westernisation.[27] In the following definition one participant calls for a fa'aSamoa that is neither hierarchical, contradictory nor hypocritical:

> Fa'aSamoa is when there is mutual respect between Samoan people. The expression of alofa must be genuine and with good intentions. Samoan cultural conventions of alofa, respect and reverence should not only be for the elders but for Samoan people who have earned it. Samoan values should be unconditional ... used in a non-hypocritical way and with good intentions. Fa'aSamoa must be flexible enough to address and meet the diverse backgrounds of Samoan people. (Lucy, born in Samoa, twenty-four years old)

The growing influences of western thought and lifestyles are a reality for contemporary young Samoan women. With the exposure to western philosophies Samoan women become 'tangled ... in the webs of power relations in modernity'.[28] While some young women do not cut themselves off completely from traditional fa'aSamoa values such as alofa (compassion) and reciprocity, their desire to have independent lifestyles is evident. The following definitions of sexuality by two of the women pose contrasting views to those of Shore, Ngan-Woo and Liu.[29] Some young Samoan women, it seems, are wanting sexual independence and an end to the controlling and disciplinary measures of male relatives toward female sexuality:

> Um, sexuality, sexuality should be an individual thing for the girl – it shouldn't be any concern for fa'aSamoa or the aiga. Samoan girls should have the choice to be virgins or not and to have choices ... to be sexually independent ... without the dominance of the Samoan males ... Sexuality for the girl is understanding her sexual needs and being able to control them if she wishes ... it's not about the control of the male, that's just male chauvinism. (Kyla, born in Samoa, twenty years old)

> I have a lot of reservations about fa'aSamoa ... It's so contradictive and hypocritical toward the women. There's this ignorant belief that Samoan men protect the Samoan girl and help them control their sexuality. This is bull, frankly, some of these guys do more harm to the girls – some of them sexually harass the girls or even rape them and then the girl gets the blame and gets the hidings ... Maybe in the olden days the guys used to protect them but today it only feeds their egos and it gets out of hand, they want to control and control not protect – big difference there ... Sexuality is a personal thing for the girl and it shouldn't be a man's business to interfere. (Susanna, born in New Zealand, nineteen years old)

How realistic is it for women located in traditional Samoan communities to become sexually independent? Much research on Samoan communities illuminates the prominent role of Samoan culture in New Zealand with the implication that many Samoan households are not being assimilated by palagi ideologies.[30] With this in mind, it is likely that many Samoan aiga in New Zealand continue to uphold conservative views of sexuality. This becomes a cultural dilemma for some women as the opportunity to learn about sexuality is rare. Many Samoan parents severely discipline daughters who have boyfriends and discourage any discussion about sex in their families for fear their daughters will engage in pre-marital sex and blemish their honour. In effect, it appears 'safer' for young Samoan women to either remain ignorant about sex and contraceptives or to have clandestine relationships without the knowledge of their parents.[31] The intention of the aiga to protect the girl from pre-marital sex is at times unrealistic and unnerving for some Samoan women as can be seen in the following comments:

> I came from a household and family where boys were an absolute no-no. The mention of 'sex' was a sin. I was going out with a guy when I was twenty seven and like was too scared to tell my parents about having a boyfriend, 'cause they'd hit the roof. So I went dating behind their backs, and like I had these funny desires I couldn't control when I was with this guy. Even at the age of twenty seven, I didn't know anything about sex, I was really naive, and, yeah, I had sex and fell pregnant. I didn't even know I was pregnant until I was around five months! Now I'm on my own, I ran away from home and am raising my child. I wish my parents weren't so overprotective of me when I was with them, it's like I struggle everyday to cope ... knowing there's a sensual side to me. (Martha, born in New Zealand, twenty nine years old)

> Sex was never ever discussed in my home. For me, being a Samoan girl was hard, especially when my body began to change, um, I didn't know what a period was, I

freaked when it happened. There was a time when I started to have these funny feelings and, yeah, I became interested in boys. But it was hard, even though my sexual drives were going berserk, I had to keep them under control, um to the point where I had to learn to deny them. It was important that I ignored them because there was no way I could've gone out with a guy without my parents' permission, and like talking to Mum about sex – please! That's asking for trouble! And then there's my brothers and uncles who are overprotective, it's impossible trying to escape ... So, even though you ... get these sexual feelings ... fa'aSamoa ... can determine when it's permissible for the girl to explore sexually or to become sexually active. For me that wasn't until I got married and twenty-eight years of age. (Malia, born in New Zealand, twenty-eight years old)

Another issue that signifies the relentless influence of Samoan culture on some Samoans in New Zealand is the 'unspoken' yet continued practice of arranged marriages. In the traditional social structure of Samoa, arranged marriages were held in the highest regard as they marked a significant cultural triumph of the woman's sexuality. More recently these elaborate ceremonies have become an exploitation of the woman's sexuality for the financial gain of her family. According to Ritchie and Ritichie this behaviour is similar to that of other Polynesian cultures in that 'new influences challenge the traditional values of ... childrearing and place greater emphasis on a money economy'.[32] Unfortunately, the young women in my research face a further predicament. Do they disobey the expectations of their aiga and face the severe consequences or defer to those of authority and escape reprimand by concealing their true feelings? The following descriptions outline both the hypocritical nature of arranged marriages and the personal, cultural and emotional dilemma some young Samoan women face to honour the wishes of their aiga and parents:

If you look at it, the only reason why there's arranged marriages and that is because of money and status. Like parents see it as making sure they don't have to worry about their daughter because she'll be all right financially, they don't have to help. They make sure the husband-to-be is comfortable financially and materialistically. They miss the whole point that love should be more important than wealth, not the other way round. (Susanna, born in New Zealand, nineteen years old)

I was eighteen when I had to marry an old minister that just came in from Samoa. My aiga didn't ask me what I wanted or what my future plans were ... I had to marry this man and that was it. I was really angry, all this time, my brothers protected me, I was forbidden to talk to boys, let alone sex! I was this chaste and virginal girl for what? So I could marry this minister? A stranger? I don't understand. I cried and cried on my wedding day, I even pleaded with my sister to cancel the wedding ... but everything was arranged and I didn't have the guts to disappoint my parents ... I couldn't dishonour their name or let the aiga down. It's a hard burden ... it's lonely being the faithful, goody-goody Samoan girl. (Josephine, born in New Zealand, twenty years old)

This is really hard for me to talk about ... my aiga planned my wedding, everything, to a Samoan minister from my dad's village. I remember, one day all my relatives came over and I just thought it was for the usual fa'alavelaves, the usual fundraising or money collecting thing … but it was to discuss my wedding. I was 19 when this happened … Thinking back I was so young, I had never had a boyfriend and I knew nothing about sex and having babies … This scared me and I kept asking why me? My aunt told me that it was a prestigious thing for a daughter to marry a minister, um, that the family would be financially well off and the daughter would be guaranteed a good lifestyle … I felt used in a way because no one ever asked how I felt, what I wanted … This is probably a harsh thing to say but I really felt exploited … I felt so powerless … I couldn't do a thing to stop it … I thought about running away, but I'd only get the rocks [get a hiding] and things will just get worse … I also thought of losing my virginity and falling pregnant so the wedding would be cancelled but, ah, it would cause further complications like, dishonouring my family publicly, um and facing disownment … [cries] … I hate my life and I hate being a minister's wife. (Trisha, born in New Zealand, twenty-four years old)

The anguished emotional state of these women clearly demonstrates the powerfulness not only of fa'aSamoa but also of the aiga. It also characterises the intense fear of ostracism from their Samoan communities and families, especially for those from rural Samoa or traditional Samoan households in New Zealand. It becomes a further burden for urban or New Zealand-born Samoan women. Their struggle to obey their aiga and traditional fa'aSamoa is particularly great as many want to be as independent as they perceive their western female peers to be. The suppression of their contempt, anger and pain is important to understand. Young Samoans are taught from early childhood to conceal their true feelings in times of adversity. This behaviour, while detrimental to the psyche of the women, is in many ways the only way they know to cope with conflict, as is shown by research on the public and private demeanour of Samoan people.[33]

The following discussions uncover some of the 'private' and 'silent' worlds of young Samoan women and display the lengths some women go to to resolve their unspoken conflicts and to become sexually independent. Although the intention of these women's actions was retaliatory, many of them were enacted for survival means – culturally, personally and spiritually:

I used to respect traditional fa'aSamoa but not any more. I think it's unfair that I have to fulfil all the cultural expectations in New Zealand and in the 1990s. I used to be the honourable daughter, I did everything my parents wanted me to do, I went to church, I stayed away from boys, I did all the fe'aus [chores], I did everything. My crime was that I fell in love with a man behind my parents' back. I was too scared to tell my parents so I used to sneak around, it was a big secret. One day, I gathered enough courage to tell my parents, I was so nervous. I got the biggest hiding of my life … they were so suspicious and they made me sound like a slut. I did everything for them and this was what I got. I left home one day and took off with this guy, I had sex and fell pregnant. Sure, I've dishonoured my parents – blah, blah – but see, fa'aSamoa should be a mutual thing. In the 1990s you cannot control female sexuality, it's no longer a realistic expectation, for me to get away, I had to disgrace them, I had to break the cycle. Sure, I feel stink but at the same time I'm at peace with myself, I can take charge of my own life now. (Patrice, born in Samoa, twenty-one years old)

My experience had to do with very strict parents. I felt trapped and I couldn't get out. And especially when I met this guy I really liked. I actually met him in New Zealand, he was Samoan and so when I went home for the holidays he came back with me 'cause he's from there and I thought I'd introduce him to my parents ... Anyway it was a complete disaster. My dad hated the idea of me having a boyfriend and he said that I was bringing shame into the family by having such a relationship ... Worst of all he made me stay in Samoa. I was not to return back to New Zealand. My mind just went crazy. It's hard to explain. I didn't even think of my parents. I wanted to prove that they were making the wrong decision by killing myself. And so I remember going out into the plantation and I had this stuff to take and I took it ... it was weird, I felt relieved 'cause it was the first thing I had done without someone saying I should or should not do it. (Madalena, born in Samoa, twenty-one years old)

I'm twenty years old and, this is hard ... I was raped by a Samoan guy when I was sixteen. He was supposed to protect me – huh – he was supposed to keep me a virgin – huh. I tried to tell my parents the truth but I got called the slut, the tart. I was punished and was sent to Samoa for two years. I had to be the obedient girl, I had to listen to my aiga and I had to earn a good reputation. It was really hard for me. I cried a lot and kept thinking back to all the things I did. I was the typical obedient Samoan girl. I always listened to my parents ... I felt betrayed, I felt guilty for no reason. Anyway, I [sobs], I couldn't take it any more. I went to the back of my aunty's place and I got some rope and tied it around the water tap by the outhouse, um the outside toilet. I was lucky ... my cousin found me dangling and I was sent to hospital. I made it and it's good to be back home in New Zealand. I've learnt a lot from this, um, I've learnt to speak out and I've learnt not to be scared any more. My parents now believe my story, but it may have been too late ... it goes to show what lengths some of us go to just to be listened to ... [sobs]. (Kataleena, born in New Zealand, twenty years old)

The difficulties facing young Samoan women within the traditional social structures of fa'aSamoa cannot be treated lightly. Many of the dilemmas raised in the above accounts reaffirm the ambiguous attitude some Samoans have toward young unmarried Samoan women and female sexuality. What does the girl have to do to convince her aiga that she has been sexually assaulted and raped by a male relative? Why do Samoans tend to side with the male and blame the young woman? Such stereotyped reactions indicate the immense challenges faced by some contemporary young Samoan women both in Samoa and New Zealand as they 'learn' their sexuality.

Future Directions

My research findings have several implications for future sex education programmes and services for young Samoan women in New Zealand. It is critical that these programmes aim to empower the women themselves by including and involving them in the development, implementation and evaluation processes. Pacific Island community fonos (forums) should be run by the youth themselves to educate health authorities and elders/aiga/parents in their respective communities about young people's perspectives on sexuality.[34] The term sexuality must be defined by young Samoan women so that services and programmes can begin from where the women themselves interpret and understand sexuality. To acknowledge the heterogeneity of young Samoan women, the overall structure of future programmes needs to be flexible, collaborative and a reflection of both Samoan and western principles and lifestyles.

The future possibilities for young Samoan women to learn effectively about sexuality in New Zealand and to define their sexualities are encouraging. There is an emerging wave of young Samoan women who are beginning to challenge traditional fa'aSamoa attitudes, and who are becoming more open in discussing matters of sex. I believe that my research is indicative of these shifts, and shows the real possibility of sexual independence and confidence for current and future generations of Samoan women.

> Giving choices enhances our capacity to attain dignity and reach our capacity as productive human beings.[35]

Notes

1   Selina Curuleca, 'The Dilemma', in Cliff Benson and Gweneth Deverell (eds), *Our World: Poems by Young Pacific Poets* (University of the South Pacific, Suva, 1991), p. 49.

2   Murray Bathgate et al., *The Health of Pacific Islands People in New Zealand: Analysis and Monitoring Report 2* (Public Health Commission, Wellington, 1994), p. 167.

3   Ibid., p. 49

4   AnneMarie Tupuola, 'Who's Educating Whom? Complexities of Doing Innovative Research' (Paper presented at the 'Speaking for Ourselves: A Critical Revisioning of New Zealand: Scholarship and the Post-Graduate Experience', Victoria University, Wellington, 1994).

5   See G. Stanley Hall, *Adolescence* (Appleton, Pasadena, 1916); Sigmund Freud, *Collected Papers, Volume 1* (The International Psycho-Analytical Press, Hogarth Press, London 1924); Margaret Mead, *Coming of Age in Samoa: A Study of Adolescence and Sex in Primitive Societies* (Penguin Books, Harmondsworth, 1943); Erik Erikson, *Identity: Youth and Crisis* (W.W. Norton, New York, 1968); Rolf Muuss, *Theories of Adolescence* (Random House, New York, 1988).

6   Katherine Dalsimer, *Female Adolescence: Psycho-Analytic Reflections on Works of Literature* (Yale University Press, New Haven, 1986), p. 42.

7   See Vijay Agnew, 'Canadian Feminism and Women of Color', *Women's Studies International Forum*, 16:3 (1993) pp. 217-227; Uma Narayan, 'The Project of Feminist Epistemology: Perspectives From a Non-Western Feminist', in Alison Jaggar and Susan Bordo (eds), *Gender/Body/Knowledge: Feminist Reconstructions of Being and Knowing* (Rutgers University Press, New Brunswick, 1990), pp. 256-72.

8   Vilisoni Hereniko, 'Indigenous Knowledge and Academic Imperialism' (Paper presented at 'Contested Ground: Knowledge and Power in Pacific Islands Studies', Hawaii, 1995).

9   See Bradd Shore, 'Sexuality and Gender in Samoa: Conceptions and Missed Conceptions', in Sherry Ortner and Harriet Whitehead (eds), *Sexual Meanings: The Cultural Construction of Gender and Sexuality* (Cambridge University Press, 1981)

pp. 192-215; Lowell Holmes, *Quest for the Real Samoa: The Mead/Freeman Controversy and Beyond* (Bergin and Garvey, South Hadley, 1987).

10 F.J. Taule'ale'ausumai, 'The Word Made Flesh', Pastoral Theology Dissertation, University of Otago, 1990, p. 12.

11 Derek Freeman, *Margaret Mead and Samoa: The Making and Unmaking of an Anthropological Myth* (Australian University Press, Canberra, 1983), p. 216.

12 Shore, p. 99.

13 Freeman, p. 236.

14 Michael Liu, 'A Politics of Identity in Western Samoa', Ph.D Thesis, University of Hawaii, 1992.

15 Freeman, pp. 228-230.

16 See Felix Ngan-Woo, *Fa'aSamoa: The World of Samoans* (New Zealand Office of Race Relations Conciliator, Auckland, 1985), p. 24; Liu.

17 Freeman, p. 236.

18 Shore, p. 201.

19 Ibid., p. 199.

20 Ibid., p. 194.

21 Maria Pallotta-Chiarolli, 'From Coercion to Choice: Second Generation Women Seeking a Personal Identity in the Italo-Australian Setting', *Journal of Intercultural Studies*, 10:1 (1989) pp. 49-63.

22 AnneMarie Tupuola, 'Fa'aSamoa in the 1990s: Young Samoan Women Speak' (Paper presented, Black Women's Institute Conference, Hawaii, 1995).

23 See Shore; Freeman, Ngan-Woo; Paul Shankman 'The Samoan Conundrum', *Canberra Anthropology*, 6:1, (1984) pp. 38-57; Liu; A. Tupuola, 'Critical Analysis of Adolescent Development: A Samoan Women's Perspective', MA Thesis, Victoria University, 1993.

24 Tupuola, 'Critical Analysis'; 'Fa'aSamoa in the 1990s'.

25 AnneMarie Tupuola, 'Raising Research Consciousness the Fa'aSamoa Way', *New Zealand Annual Review of Education*, 3 (1993), pp. 175-189.

26 Tupuola, 'Critical Analysis of Adolescent Development', pp. 49-82.

27 See Taule'ale'ausumai, 'The Word'; Malani Anae, 'On the Hyphen: A New Zealand-Born Perspective', Unpublished Paper, 1995.

28 Liu, p. 187.

29 Shore; Ngan-Woo; Liu.

30 See David Pitt and Cluny Macpherson, *Emerging Pluralism: Samoan Community in New Zealand* (Longman Paul, Auckland, 1974); Jane Ritchie and James Ritichie, *Growing Up in Polynesia* (George Allen & Unwin, Sydney, 1979); Cluny Macpherson, 'On the Future of Samoan Ethnicity in New Zealand', in Paul Spoonley *et al.*, (eds), *Tauiwi: Racism and Ethnicity* (Dunmore Press, Palmerston North, 1984).

31 R. Bright, 'Sexuality Education in Aotearoa: Is it Appropriate for the Needs of Maori and Samoan Women?', BA (Hons) Research Project, Victoria University, 1994.

32 Ritchie and Ritichie, p. 15.

33 See Shore; Freeman; Holmes; Colin Tukitonga, 'The Health of Pacific Island People in New Zealand', Unpublished Report for New Zealand College of Community Medicine Examination, 1990; Lanuola Asiasiga, 'Abortion and Pacific Islands Women: Pilot Study for the New Zealand Family Planning Association', Wellington, 1994.

34 Bright, p. 39.

35 Terri Jewell (ed.), *The Black Woman's Gumbo Ya-Ya: Quotations by Black Women* (The Crossing Press, Watsonville, 1993), p. 63.

FIVE

Gender and Work in Fiji:
Constraints to Re-negotiation

JACQUELINE LECKIE

As globalisation becomes more pervasive in the Pacific Islands, so it is rapidly influencing women's lives and work patterns. Increasing numbers of women are dependent on paid employment, both in less structured sectors and in the formal labour market. To what extent are gender categories and identities being reconstructed as women negotiate their working lives? This essay[1] explores the 'messy realities'[2] in Fiji where, despite seemingly rigid ethnic boundaries and a strong legacy of colonisation and tradition, women's identities are often more fractured than these structures might imply. This reflects tumultuous changes of the past decade from political upheavals, including military coups, economic hardship and structural adjustment. Work in highly feminised sectors is examined, showing links between shifting cultural and ethnic identities, economic and political restructuring, state policies, the workplace, family and community.[3] In this essay, these contexts are discussed with reference to three working women in contemporary Fiji. Their gender identities and stereotypes override more specific constraints these women have faced in re-negotiating their work situations.

Mele[4] is the oldest of the three, and in 1996, on reaching the mandatory retirement age of fifty-five, left her nursing career. Her family were part of the emergent Fijian middle class that challenged chiefly politics during the late twentieth century. Education and service were strong family values for Mele's minister grandfather, school teacher mother, and aunt, also a nurse. Mele grew up living in different communities and with strong independent female role models. Despite this, she was never promoted above the level of staff nurse. Partly this reflected her family commitments, which Mele sees as her choice. She resigned from nursing aged twenty four to marry a senior civil servant but resumed paid work in a library which allowed her to expand her reading and knowledge. In 1981 she returned to nursing at age forty. Mele became frustrated at the lack of specialised training and transfers 'at whim' that impeded promotion. Her maturity and awareness of workplace and political issues led her to take a proactive role in her union and in a prominent nurses' strike in 1990. By then her children were all well educated and today work in professional occupations or in business.

Asena[5] was born in 1970 and spent her childhood and school years in a village in the Rewa Delta, near Suva. She assumed that, like her mother, she would continue with subsistence gardening and fishing. Asena's transition from child to adult had been swift; by age twenty two she had two children. This coincided with military coups in 1987 and subsequent 'structural adjustment'. Both promised better opportunities for indigenous Fijians but Asena experienced mainly economic hardship. There were no outlets for earning cash in the village. Previously her husband may have secured work in Suva but with rising unemployment and retrenchment in the public and private sectors after 1987 he could not provide for his family. The onus for this fell on Asena, but it was a role she partly welcomed, as it offered some independence. Her independence was secondary to earning income to support her children and husband. Asena left her children with her husband's mother in the village, visiting them at weekends. Like many new female migrants from rural Fiji, through kinship networks, Asena became a paid domestic worker.[6] Although earning $35 a week she was bored and lonely, so sought employment in Fiji's growth area: export garment production. In 1994 she was a 'seam-buster', earning 75 cents an hour to feed as many dress collar shirts as possible into the machine.

Asena's husband joined her in Suva to share a small apartment in a working class suburb with her parents and a young male cousin. The latter was also hired at the same factory as Asena but did not contribute to household income or remit money to the village. As her male family members in Suva shun housework, Asena's day begins around 4.30 a.m. preparing the family's breakfast, and doing washing and ironing. Factory work begins at 7.45 a.m. with a fifteen minute break for tea and thirty minutes for lunch. She usually finishes at 5 p.m. but often works overtime, including Saturdays, at the same rate. In the evening Asena resumes domestic duties. Despite the long hours in formal employment, her wages are inadequate to meet her family's expenses. One week her wages were arbitrarily deducted. This was at United Apparel, the recipient of the Textile, Clothing and Footwear Award, in Fiji's Prime Minister's Exporter of the Year competition in 1993.

Sita, an Indo-Fijian, is thirty-one years old and lives on a sugar cane farm in Vanua Levu with her husband, three children, mother-in-law and her husband's brother's family.[7] She grew up with her eight brothers and three sisters on a 50-acre family cane farm, situated near town. Sita was expected to help with domestic work and subsistence agriculture but hoped to avoid the destiny of her mother and aunties. She married in 1985 at the age of twenty-one to join her husband's family. Her new family is not as financially secure as her birth family and can not afford to hire farm labourers. Besides domestic work, Sita labours extensively in subsistence and sugarcane farming. During busy periods she will rise at 4 a.m. and not rest before 10 p.m.

Mele, Asena and Sita are women workers with much in common, especially when their lives are considered against the global diversity of gender and work. They are all citizens of Fiji. Workers there share a history of colonisation by Britain between 1874–1970, which left differing implications for gender and other identities, especially ethnicity. Mele, Sita and Asena are not necessarily stereotypes of women workers but their lives reflect a slice of the complexities of women's lives. This essay emphasises gender but also how this is reinforced by dynamics of ethnicity and class.[8]

Although sharing much, there are differences in the highly feminised employment sectors where these women work, reflecting shifting cultural and ethnic identities, expectations of family and community, workplace conditions and the impact of local and global politics and economics. These in turn bear upon the forms and extent to which the women can re-negotiate gender expectations and roles. Mele as a health worker is part of Fiji's established public sector. The nursing profession has marked indigenous female participation and is strongly unionised. Factory production for the global market is new not only to Asena but also to Fiji. This sector is highly feminised and multiethnic with shifting unionisation and workplace resistance from very overt to weak. The sector Sita works in, farming, is one of Fiji's oldest work sectors. Women's participation has been largely unrecognised. Most sugar cane farms were run by Indo-Fijians but now more indigenous Fijians are involved in cash cropping. Women cane workers are collectively unorganised.

The Setting of Women's Work in Fiji

In the written record of labour in Fiji[9] women's role appears minuscule because until the late twentieth century women's participation in paid work was slight. Within Fiji's formal workforce, women comprised 14 per cent in 1970, increasing to 30.5 per cent by 1993.[10] This contribution to Fiji's recorded economy requires closer attention. Historical roots from the nineteenth century established many of the parameters for women's choices in the paid workforce a century later. Early colonial labour patterns also set Fiji's ethnic dynamics that still reinforce gendered structures of domination and subordination. Before examining the complexities within the sectors Mele, Asena and Sita work in, we need to sketch their common but fractured background.

Mele and Asena work in the formal sector of Fiji's economy, in government and manufacturing, where two-thirds of women in paid labour are employed. Considerable numbers of women also work in the tourism, wholesale, retail and financial sectors.[11] Asena's is a relatively new sector but Mele and Sita's work, nursing and farming, have been major options for women throughout the colonial and post-colonial periods.

For centuries, women, along with men, were crop producers in Pacific Islands societies. Women's agricultural roles have not diminished but very few are classified or identify as farmers. Fiji's 1991 agricultural census recorded 4857 individual women as farmers. This represented only 5.2 per cent of all farmers but women's role is much greater as subsistence and unpaid agricultural labourers.

One reason for this anomaly is that much of this work has been slotted into domestic work. Horticultural work was also regarded as coming 'naturally' to indigenous Fijians. In the Pacific, non-cash farming is often labelled 'gardening' which falsely has become equated with 'domestic work' or a 'hobby'. However an overriding determinant of women's location in agricultural work came from the colonial political economy that developed in Fiji.

Fiji's participation in the global economy began with the extraction of luxury goods such as sandalwood, bêche de mer and coconut oil during the first half of the nineteenth century. Women's labour would have been essential to providing food and services, including prostitution. After cession to Britain, Fiji became dependant on the export of raw sugar, with copra and later gold as exports of fluctuating significance. From 1879–1920 sugarcane was predominantly produced on plantations that relied upon the intensive cheap labour of indentured Indian workers (*Girmitiyas*). This instigated Fiji's multiethnic society, and by World War II Indo-Fijians constituted the largest ethnic group of the colony's population. This percentage declined to 45 per cent after 1987 due to emigration and lower birth rates among indigenous Fijians.

How did the plantation economy cross over into the politics of gender as well as ethnicity? Regulations designated 40 per cent of indentured emigrants be women[12]; their labour costs were cheaper than men's and unpaid labour was crucial to the care and reproduction of the current and future workforce. This became evident after the last indenture in 1920 when production shifted from plantations to small family farms. Cane contracts were only issued to married men but farms of 10–15 acres were too small to provide an adequate living for extended families. The Colonial Sugar Refining Company (CSR) therefore had a labour supply to work in the mills, as harvesting gangs and other farm work. CSR offered the pretence of farmers' autonomy, while retaining control of production through off-loading production costs. After independence the company withdrew from Fiji but the industry continued to be a major exporter and employer under the Fiji Sugar Corporation (FSC).

Colonial policies had the effect of limiting indigenous Fijians to subsistence work, but there was far greater indigenous participation in paid work than was publicly recognised.[13] Women's village, fishing and horticultural work was not measured, although essential for financial and community obligations. Customary controls on women's geographical and occupational mobility were strengthened by colonial regulations.[14] Villages constituted a labour reserve where women's labour met many of the costs of the maintenance and reproduction of the workforce.

Women's constricted involvement in Fiji's paid workforce continued after political independence. Most work remained unrecorded, casual or unregulated, as domestic workers, market vendors, sex workers or in family businesses or farms. As throughout the world, a small but increasing number of workers became drawn into the monetised economy during World War II and by 1960 women were working in factories.[15]

After independence in 1970, women's formal employment opportunities were mainly in the public, retailing, financial and tourism sectors. The economic slump of the 1980s gave way to a new growth area of employment that sought cheap female labour: export manufacturing. International lending agencies, such as the World Bank, and local entrepreneurs and politicians, advocated Fiji follow global patterns of industrial restructuring and export-orientated manufacturing. In Fiji this brought (13 year) tax free factories, with much overseas investment. The economic crisis caused by Fiji's military coups in 1987 fast-tracked restructuring and provided state coercion against workers' opposition. Structural adjustment included currency devaluation, external trade liberalisation and internal deregulation to promote internationally competitive industries.[16]

Since 1988 garment manufacturing has been Fiji's main employment growth area and by 1990, the biggest export after sugar. In 1996 an estimated 14,000 workers, the majority women, were in garment manufacturing. In 1986 women comprised only 9.7 per cent of the manufacturing labour force but now account for 50 per cent, equating to 14 per cent of formal sector employment.[17]

Fiji's Florence Nightingales

Fiji's public service has almost equal numbers of men and women. Women comprise 45 per cent of Fiji's civil servants. Closer inspection indicates a clear gender segmentation by sector and level, with females concentrated in health and education.[18] In 1978 women represented only 20 per cent of civil servants outside teaching and nursing.[19] In 1996, 48 per cent of all female civil servants were employed in the Ministry of Education, Women and Culture. A third of female public servants comprised approximately 60 per cent of all health workers, mostly as nurses.[20] Males were only recently admitted into nursing and constitute about 3 per cent of Fiji's nurses. The range of salaries within the nursing division is narrow so that most graduates are restricted to earning between $7000 and $9000. Although women occupy senior positions in the nursing division, there are few of these, creating a 'bottleneck' career structure.[21] Similarly in education, and other sectors of the civil service, women are clustered at the lower paid levels; only 8 per cent of upper positions, 20 per cent of middle posts and 48 per cent at lower levels.[22]

Women were unlikely to pursue a skilled profession in colonial Fiji with the exceptions of teaching and nursing. Today, nurses represent one of the most under-paid and overworked professions in Fiji. However, competition for selection in the annual intake of 120 nursing students remains fierce, despite low pay, heavy workloads and strict regulations on conduct, attitude and academic achievement. Historical antecedents bear on the present and for several decades have led to protests about fair recompense and recognition of nurses' work.

Harriet Bradley's description of health services in Britain as a 'highly differentiated structure of hierarchies'[23] applies to Fiji. These hierarchies have been reinforced along colonial, ethnic, age, family, educational but mostly gender lines. Fiji's contemporary nursing practices and ideology have been shaped by the 'Nightingale tradition', reproduced through Australian and New Zealand nursing systems. This promotes nursing not only as a respectable occupation for 'ladies' but also as a regulated middle class career. Nightingale's advocacy was based on a notion of differentiated male and female worlds where nursing should be an autonomous female preserve.[24] This was easily inculcated by indigenous Fijians, partly because of women's traditional healing roles and missionary examples of nursing and femininity. In Indo-Fijian communities nursing was generally considered an unclean and very low status occupation, previously associated with the *dai* or midwife.[25] Parents were extremely reluctant to allow daughters to nurse male patients. Most Indo-Fijian nurses in the earlier colonial years were educated or trained in a Christian school or hospital. The low status of nursing for Indo-Fijian women persisted after independence although as young women gained higher education they challenged negative stereotypes. Today, nursing is an acceptable career for Indo-Fijian women, especially as it offers qualifications that can be marketed abroad by migrants.

Many nurses in Fiji attribute their unsatisfactory pay and working conditions to the way the occupation is an extension of gender relations. Former Fiji Nursing Association secretary Kiti Vatanimoto stressed that Fijian cultures reinforced gender inequality:

> Customs and traditions have continued to place women in an inferior position. This cultural background colours the attitude of the Ministry of Health, male society as a whole, in regard to nurses and their problems. From time immemorial nurses in Fiji have generally accepted their inferior role as an integral part of their existence.[26]

The health profession in Europe became differentiated into the male sphere of curing and the female sphere of caring, with these roles reflecting family relationships and identities.[27] Curing required learning but caring apparently came naturally to women so was nurtured, as much as trained. Today health professionals are re-negotiating this, but old stereotypes are resistant. Nightingale's vision of nursing as an extension of mothering, as a natural, biological expression of femininity, is replicated by many nurses in Fiji. This role is also couched in Christian terms. Some nurses are resigned to their poor pay because: 'Nursing is a vocation ... real calling ... healing hands in place of Jesus. The Lord will reward you.' However some nurses are aware that caring is inevitably linked to their biological, cultural or spiritual destinies: nurses are: 'a health care giver, soothe dying, bring life into the world.'[28]

In the Shadows of Fiji's 'Showpiece': Export Manufacturing

Stereotypes about women and work were prominent in the rapid growth of the garments industry. Ingrained gender and cultural stereotypes were the rationale for preferentially employing women and offering inferior pay and working conditions to workers in comparable industries. Minimum wages in Fiji's garments industry during 1997 were 90 cents for trainees and $1.10 after that. Most workers earn between $30–$40 a week. The industry has long working hours, averaging 60 hours a week in 1991.[29] Overtime payments are frequently avoided, health and safety records are often poor and workers have lost their jobs over taking leave for maternity, illness or childcare. Employers will transfer workers to another enterprise to avoid paying full-rates after a six month training period.

Instead of the feminine attribute of caring, other feminine skills such as dexterity, 'nimble fingers' and docility have been cited to explain women's suitability as garment workers.[30] More significantly, most of these workers are new to factory production with no experience of union protection.

Low pay has been justified by employers and the state because women are not perceived as primary wage earners while men are entitled to a 'family wage'. This is the notion of women working for personal motives: 'lipstick', 'pin money', self fulfilment or social interaction.[31] Women workers acknowledge these incentives but realise that their income has become essential and not simply supplementary to the male 'breadwinner's'. A 1993 survey of 260 female garment workers found one third to be sole income earners.[32] Ironically, in Asena's family, her male cousin works for 'fun money'.

Christy Harrington found that not only is women's participation in Fiji's labour market, and explicitly the garments industry, best understood in terms of gender, but there is also a clear gendered division of labour in the factory. Men's and women's tasks tend to be segmented according to different classifications of skill and remuneration. In many factories men occupy most of the managerial and supervisory roles, work on fully automated machines and in the 'skilled' cutting sections.[33]

Far from the Factories: Women in Farm Production

Generally, in most farming households there is a fairly fixed gender division of labour. In Sita's family, women work up to sixteen hours a day with responsibility for work considered 'domestic': food preparation and serving, processing coconut oil, spices and preserves, washing clothes, dishes, cleaning, carrying water, most child care, animal care and vegetable gardening. Women also plant, weed and fertilise cane. Their double shift of farm and domestic work involves a multiplicity of tasks that are often simultaneous – for example, child care while weeding the cane field. Researchers in other Pacific Islands are recognising women's contiguous participation in cash cropping, informal trading, subsistence, culture and community activities.[34]

Men in Sita's family focus on one farming task or, if available, off-farm work. Men and women both plant and fertilise crops but men only occasionally weed. When men are harvesting cane they have little involvement in subsistence agriculture. Meanwhile women's work expands dramatically when providing meals for the harvesting gang and if cane cutters live on the farm.

Sue Carswell found the division of labour not always fixed but mediated by labour availability. Contrary to the perceptions of senior FSC officials, women, especially in poorer families, work in the fields and harvest cane. When families are predominantly male, younger boys are expected to help with domestic chores. Expectations about age and labour intersect with gender. Sex-typing of work roles begins with girls helping in both domestic and farm work while boys concentrate on farming.

It is difficult to generalise about gender and decision-making on family farms. Many decisions about harvesting and planting are outside the family, decided by FSC. Negotiation of this is through farmers' organisations. Sita's life story reflects the authority accorded to her father and brothers but this obscures the influence women may covertly have.

More specific gender divisions apply with access to state and financial support for female farmers. Although women's labour has sustained subsistence farming and cash cropping, there has been little recognition, external advice or access to new farming equipment. This 'affects not only the subsistence situation of rural families but also employability of women in agricultural activities.'[35] Agricultural extension officers rarely consult women on farms, and in 1993 only 9 per cent of such officers were female. Many women still have considerable difficulty in securing loans, lacking not only collateral and deposits but also confidence. During 1993, 56 per cent of Fiji Development Loans went to agriculture but only 11 per cent were exclusively secured by women.[36]

Opportunities for off-farm labour are also gendered throughout Fiji, depending on access to industrial or tourist centres. Single urban female migration is not morally acceptable in some Indo-Fijian families. Migration also depletes domestic and farm labour for families not living in a communal village.[37] In Sita's region, off-farm work opportunities are particularly limited for women. There are some informal sector cash and exchange opportunities for weaving baskets and mats, crocheting and sewing. Food and labour for planting rice and cane are reciprocated among families. Although negative attitudes persist about Indo-Fijian women in rural communities participating in formal work, economic necessity and individual choice are pushing an increasing number into seeking off-farm employment.

Gender Ideologies, Education and Expectations

Ingrained gender ideologies in Fiji's communities channel women's entry into particular sectors of the labour market and limit their ability to re-negotiate gender and work. How have Hindu, Muslim and Christian cultures, and ethnic, gender and class stereotypes, structured partly through colonialism, mediated this? One intersection has been education.

The education system reproduces gendered stereotypes about work. Missionary ideals of femininity and appropriate education were powerful influences in the Pacific Islands.[38] Past trends of channelling women into 'feminine' caring or service industries have persisted.

Like many women, Mele, Sita and Asena's occupational aspirations and opportunities were partly circumscribed by their formal education, which was shaped by economic constraints, state policies and cultural expectations. Mele was able to acquire a higher standard of education, like many nurses, at boarding school. This was at Ballantine, a school which 'processed' potential nurses and teachers. Several Fijian nurses recall a relatively easy transition, often with the same peer group, from secondary school to nursing school to hospital work. This strongly communal but also hierarchical lifestyle carried over from living together at boarding school to nursing hostels.

Colonial authorities fostered ethnically and gendered segregated education. For the Fijian elite this was through boarding schools where a communal camaraderie was encouraged provided it was tempered with 'European discipline'. Like schooling opportunity, the nursing hierarchy was structured on a racial basis.[39] Racial and colonial lines demarcated the nursing hierarchy. Fijian women were trained as midwives and district nurses with most specialised and senior positions reserved for white expatriates until the 1960s. Nursing students were divided into either the 'New Zealand class' or the 'colonial class' to respectively qualify as a New Zealand or Fiji nurse. The New Zealand class members were groomed to assume senior positions.[40]

It might appear that Mele was moulded into a conservative, gendered, occupational position, but she later utilised this to widen her options and education. In contrast Sita's secondary schooling prepared her for broader career options but her father and husband vetoed this. Nursing training has enforced a delay in marriage and child bearing for thousands of Fijian women. Their identity as paid workers is established before their identity as mothers and wives. Mele resigned from nursing after the birth of her first child but continued with intellectual and community pursuits before resuming nursing. Compared to other occupations in Fiji, nursing offered more flexibility for negotiating family life with formal employment but this compromise has reinforced low salaries and limited career paths for nurses. Nursing encompasses the contradictory interplay of domestic and work identities but with the rationale that nurses should be grateful to have a profession.

Both economic and cultural pressures have limited women's formal education and severely restricted employment opportunities.

> It remains a standard practice that a wife subordinates career development to that of her husband, and the education of daughters to that of the sons. Consequently, equality of opportunity and treatment in training and education and employment is also dependent on a household's expectations of men's and women's roles in society.[41]

Asena's village education, with less than two years senior schooling, offered fewer educational and occupational possibilities, compared to Mele. Their work narratives reiterate the division of education between boarding and village schools, through shaping hierarchies of occupation and identity. Asena and her teachers assumed her future would be as a 'village housewife' but in contemporary Fiji women are increasingly income earners which often draws them from the village. Asena's husband is unemployed so she has taken primary responsibility for the family's economic welfare.[42] This was virtually impossible in the village, and with her limited education, Asena had few choices in Suva's labour market.

During the colonial period, Indo-Fijian girls were especially disadvantaged in access to schooling. Education was, and still is, not compulsory and is costly for families in Fiji. Economic pressures and gender stereotypes limited girls' educational opportunities. Indo-Fijian women had much lower literacy rates than indigenous women and Indian men until the 1950s.[43] Indo-Fijian parents' preference to marry daughters by fifteen years impeded women's education. In 1936, 84 per cent of Indian women aged nineteen were married compared to 10 per cent of indigenous Fijian women.[44] Fifty years later, Sita observed little change in her vicinity:

> The girls should be only educated up to class eight, [age thirteen] then keep two or three years home, stay home, just get some education in cooking food and how to put their houses and then seventeen, eighteen they marry.

The average age at marriage for Indo-Fijian women in 1989 was twenty, still lower than Indo-Fijian men (twenty-four) and indigenous Fijians (twenty-three for women and twenty-seven for men).[45]

Indo-Fijian women's educational levels have risen markedly during past decades but as Sita's life illustrates this may not necessarily translate into attaining a career. Her education to Fiji's senior level (Form 7) was longer than that of Asena and Mele. After leaving school she completed a stenography course but her father considered the clerical work she sought unsuitable. Undeterred, Sita applied to train as an air flight attendant, then as a nurse, but because she was under twenty years required her father's consent. He refused to sign either form. When Sita did gain legal majority at twenty one years her father arranged her career as a wife.

Ironically, unpaid farm work is acceptable for women in Sita's locality but pursuing this as a career has been considered inappropriate for women.

Community constraints are replicated at the wider state level with poor acknowledgement of women's farming skills in educational syllabi and agricultural extension programmes. Before 1983 the intake of women at the Fiji College of Agriculture was restricted to two, and in 1988 no females were enrolled there.[46] Wider educational equity is more positive. Today relatively high levels of females and males enrol and graduate from Fiji's primary and secondary schools while women comprise 45 per cent of students at the University of the South Pacific.[47] Many women in Fiji have high educational achievements but this is inadequately developed in the workplace.

Control and Resistance

Women's experience of control and resistance in relation to employment takes many forms. Each woman has come up against specific restrictions. Sita especially faced the culturally-bound constraints of family; Mele experienced the frustrating constraints of politics, but for Asena and an increasing number of women in the South Pacific, the hopeless constraints of poverty were overriding. The women's life-stories show these constraints are often shared so that any re-negotiation of gender, work and power in Fiji will need to cover much common ground.

Every time Sita was offered a job her father or husband refused to consent. Such control is complex and reinforced through personal ties of love and loyalty, fear of non-acceptance or bringing shame to the family but also can be through psychological and physical abuse. The local community may indirectly condone these restraints and perpetuate traditional gender roles. Sita's father arranged her marriage because he thought this would be the best life for her and it was his responsibility to pass her on to the care of a husband and his family. After her father forbade her to go nursing Sita 'really cried for the work and still I don't go well now. I didn't eat food for, I think, about a week.' Sita's husband did not allow her to work outside the farm when a relative at a nearby school asked her to assist with teaching. Instead she has endured family control to conform to gendered and cultural expectations of primarily identifying as a respectable, 'dependent' wife and mother. She did resist this destiny through unsuccessful attempts to apply for jobs.

Mele had a supportive family environment for her career choices. Rather than facing employment restraints at home, on her return to nursing she found the state held up stereotypes of family and caring, to deny better wages and conditions. Ironically her resignation from the public service was because she chose to become a wife and mother; until 1975 married female civil servants were required to resign from permanent employment within the civil service. They could reapply but in the process broke their service record and were usually reappointed at the same or a lower grade.

Family constraints have affected Mele's peers in other ways as well. For instance, marriage ties have influenced industrial relations. During the nurses' strike of 1990, a senior nurse on strike found herself in an ambivalent position and under pressure to keep working because her husband was a local senior medical officer with political and personal connections with government leaders.[48] Some nurses did not inform their husbands that they were striking, for fear of opposition.

Mele's workplace was also affected by pay inequalities. Ideology about men's responsibilities for family incomes has been central to gender pay inequality. As noted, garment employers fell back on this assumption to justify wages for women that could not support a family. Female public sector workers were similarly discriminated against when seeking promotions and job allowances. For example, until the early 1980s, married female civil servants were not entitled to government quarters[49] which affected promotions because women could not gain experience in rural posts. A permanent secretary clearly reflected prevailing attitudes about gender, work and family when he asserted in 1977 that women were not entitled to such housing as it was the 'responsibility of the husband to fend for the family'.[50] Interruptions due to child-bearing were another excuse for not promoting women. Stereotypes about gender and authority persist. When a female civil servant appealed against a male being promoted over her, she was asked: 'Do you think junior officers and members of the public would accept a woman as a supervising officer in this society?'[51]

Mele and co-workers were adamant that political pressure on union activities impeded opportunities for promotion and training. After the 1990 nurses' strike, reports of victimisation were common, including false allegations about striking nurses and claims of favouritism with duties, promotions, training and leave being dispensed to wives and close relatives of senior officials in the Ministry of Health, who had not taken strike action.[52] Some senior nursing officers with managerial qualifications and skills, it was asserted, were transferred and replaced by less skilled nurses.

Although nurses like Mele receive higher incomes than garment workers like Asena, they have faced growing economic pressures and increasingly are household heads. Compassionate motives may be dominant when many women begin nursing, but Fiji's rising cost of living has made nurses more acutely aware of the relative economic value of their labour and income.

As an urban factory worker, Asena's experiences are shared by an increasing number of women in the Asia-Pacific region entering the labour force. She has taken responsibility for her family's livelihood to endure exploitative pay and working conditions. The growing number of rural Fijians living in or vulnerable to poverty has been a catalyst in urban migration and adds to the number of urban poor. As noted with Sita, paid employment opportunities in cane-growing areas tend to favour men. In 1993 one in three rural households were estimated to live below the poverty line,[53] while between 1989–1991 the percentage of poor urban households doubled from 20 to 40 per cent.[54] Overall, at least a quarter of Fiji's population is estimated to be living in poverty.[55]

The global trend of women's vulnerability to poverty includes Fiji. In the early 1980s this was partly because of limited employment opportunities for women. By the late 1980s, the 'economic miracle' of export manufacturing opened up jobs for women, but with pay rates that trapped many women into a lifetime of poverty. Jenny Bryant found 55.5 per cent of Fiji's female headed households lived in poverty and among all poor households, 20 per cent were headed by women.[56] These proportions have increased. Poor women are extremely vulnerable to insecure employment and this mitigates against being assertive and organising in the workplace. Likewise garment workers have reported victimisation because of their union activities. Recalcitrant garment workers faced dismissal, pay cuts or psychological and physical abuse.[57] Supervisors sometimes 'belittle' workers by calling them 'worthless because their work is worthless.' The inflicting of public shame is highly distressing in many Pacific cultures. Shaming can take place with productivity markers, such as different coloured cards, displayed on a worker's machine.[58] The state has been resistant to investigation or amendment of grievances; a key attraction of Fiji's tax- free factories was the military regime's promise that unions would be banned.

Collective Resistance

Women's networks, involvement and solidarity have been vital in workers' protests and political and union representation in Fiji. Women's direct participation in unions began in the public sector in teaching, the civil service and nursing. When compared to many other Pacific Islands workers, nurses are strongly unionised with 71 per cent being members of Fiji Nursing Association (FNA).[59] Its predecessor, the Fiji Nurses' Union, founded in 1956 by locally trained nurses, had support from colonial officials and met little opposition to recognition by government in 1977.

There has been considerable contestation among nurses about the association's identity and methods. An extreme minority is opposed to the association identifying as a union or pursuing overt resistance. Another pole considers FNA to be weak with little 'bite'. One organiser complained of members' resistance to any discourse smacking of feminist or women's perspectives. The successful week-long strike in 1990 evoked more commonly held contradictory views on unionism and industrial action. A nursing sister who went on strike:

> inside felt guilty … about this sad occasion … doesn't like the term trade union … FNA is an association, it's unprofessional to go on strike, the ministry should look after nurses and their welfare.

The strike's central issue, state provision of safe transport for nurses on shift work, was first raised almost twenty years ago.[60] Government resistance to union requests for transport provisions and the frustration expressed by nurses indicated deeper problems between health workers and management: low salaries, understaffing, inadequate promotions and arbitrary transfers.

> The poor wages of the nurse, that started getting to me, I think after about three years, the fourth year I started realising we were working so hard, we are doing shift work, breaking our backs to implement government polices that they made up, they're at the top. I started thinking here is me carrying out the policies that they make yet I have no say in their policy making. They are very quick to lay down policies, this, that, with no regards with who is ever going to run it and they come up with new policies, new services, every year there is something that they want us to run new. But the pay is not renewed or anything. You ask people, we are not getting enough for this.

This was not the first industrial action taken by nurses. In 1959, forty six nurses at Lautoka hospital went on a three day strike over workplace grievances.[61] FNA was not registered as a union and had few bargaining rights, so most strikers 'absconded'. Later discontent was more public with an overtime ban and a vocal protest march through Suva in 1983.[62] The assumed passive identity of nurses has not equated with a lack of collective organisation.

Nurses sometimes take sick leave as a form of resistance but more often this indicates stress. The nursing establishment has not encouraged overt workplace resistance but rather the seeking of solace through the Nurses' Christian Fellowship. One nursing sister observed generational differences in forms of coping:

> A few of them turn to God but I don't think that they are fully satisfied by their turning to God. When you look at it, the older ones, I don't know how they are dealing with their stress, I think they have got to a stage of learned helplessness. Where they couldn't be bothered whether the patient gets their temperature taken or not … other people have reached stages whereby they just learn to go on but I think with the young ones, thirty-five and under … most would turn to alcohol and to nicotine.

The two nursing welfare institutions, the union and Christian fellowship have less relevance to Hindu and Muslim nurses.[63] Many identify FNA as 'Fijianised' and increasingly resist their employment situation by opting out, seeking alternative paid work or emigrating.

In contrast to nurses, garment workers faced state opposition to collective representation and bargaining. The administration backed down on earlier plans to bar unions from tax free factories. The Fiji Association of Garment Workers was registered in 1989 but employers strongly resisted recognition. Garment workers went on strike during 1990–1.[64] Besides union recognition, issues included low wages averaging $20 a week, inadequate toilet facilities, excessively heavy work, overtime without extra payment or transport being provided, body searches for missing items and no sick and annual leave or tea breaks.[65]

They're treating us like slaves. It gets so hot and stuffy in there. It just gets unbearable having to work without proper ventilation and it's ridiculous not being allowed to go to the toilets when you want to.[66]

Although industrial unrest still simmers in Fiji's garment industry, overt militancy has not been sustained. Membership of the garment workers' union has dropped from 2000 to less than 700. Only two out of over 200 firms recognise the union for bargaining purposes.

Other forms of resistance are more pervasive, notably absenteeism, industrial sabotage and low productivity. Harrington reported women smearing lipstick on clothes or 'creatively' sewing garments, in protest. Forsyth attributed the high labour turnover to 'an adversarial and unhappy environment'.[67] Labour turnover may also reflect employer tactics of keeping costs low by dismissing employees qualifying for full pay rates.

Farming women like Sita have no formal outlets to negotiate their working conditions. The cane cutting gang deals with disputes, and growers (usually the male household head) have union representatives. Women farm workers 'resist' their workload covertly; for example, through sickness, 'absconding' to an aunty's house, or religious commitments.[68]

Conclusion: Family and Future Global Constraints

Through snippets of the lives of Mele, Asena and Sita, we see how gender ideology and the division of labour in Fiji reflect cultural and family values, colonial ideologies and institutions, and more contemporary economic and political restructuring. Although their work is differentiated by sector, income, and degrees and forms of autonomy, they share inadequate working situations and uncertain futures. The constraints to renegotiating their situations differ for each woman, according to time, place, class, age, ethnicity, cultural expectations and the political economy.

All three women identify how their feminine and cultural roles limit choices for them and their children. Sita's work and identity as a farm worker have been under-recognised and gained little political advocacy despite such work being highly pivotal in economic and political restructuring, land tenure, economic diversification and the future of Fiji's sugar industry. Fiji has a sugar quota arrangement with the European Union under the Lomé Agreement but prices will drastically fall. Simultaneously most Indo-Fijian sugar growers face renewals of farm leases from crown or Fijian-owned land. These transitions and upheavals are raising problems for the future of household and community relations. The Ministry of Agriculture, Forestry and Fisheries, and ALTA[69] extension services have begun to recognise the importance of women's contribution to farming by recruiting more female officers, holding gender awareness staff courses and incorporating women into extension programmes.[70] Occupational diversification into tourism, manufacturing, market vending and service industries are also being advocated by state agencies. Earlier preferences among farming families for daughters to remain on farms are rapidly changing as Indo-Fijian farming families face an insecure future. Sita strongly encourages both her daughter and sons to achieve at school: 'education is their ticket out of poverty'. She expects her daughter to pursue a career and have the choice of overseas emigration but perceives little change for herself: 'Myself I have to stay here with my husband.' Sita's obsession with her children's future also stems from the political insecurity of her ethnic group.

Public sector 'reforms' have been a cornerstone of Fiji's structural adjustment programme. Key changes have been fiscal cuts, privatisation and corporatisation of government departments. This has major implications for female employees as a high proportion are concentrated in the public sector. Inadequate staffing levels compound frustration over career prospects and skills' recognition. One of Mele's successors realised 'her salary was lousy because the bosses in the Medical Department were not fighting but were … cost-cutting on nursing.' Regardless of awareness of political pressures in the public sector this young assertive nurse still identified gender as a future hurdle: 'We are women, can't fight.'

Asena works in a sector seemingly more modern and globally integrated than that of Sita or Mele. The coups promised to alleviate her situation as a disadvantaged Fijian. Yet her ability to re-negotiate her employment situation is futile. She works to provide economic security for her current and probable future children. Her domestic work will increase along with financial responsibilities if her husband remains unemployed. Pay levels in Fiji are unlikely to greatly increase, as Fiji looses preferential access to markets in Australia, New Zealand with the demise of SPARTECA (South Pacific Regional Trade and Economic Co-operation Agreement), and to the USA with the gradual elimination of the Multi Fibre Agreement under the Uruguay Round of GATT (General Agreement on Tariffs and Trade).[71] Fiji's manufacturing exports already face competition from lower cost suppliers in Asia. Another trend is the hiring of foreign labour from China, Taiwan and the Philippines. Globalisation is limiting Asena's ability to negotiate her future. It is likely she will continue to rely on 'feminine attributes' to find low-paid or casual work in Fiji's growing service industry.

Women in Fiji share a common gender identity but this is fractured by ethnicity, class, religion, age and education. Global restructuring is impacting on their working lives, and has already influenced employment options and defines current conditions. This also raises many questions with uncertain answers about the future of women and work in the Pacific. Some certainty is clear: the persistence of gender and ethnic ideologies in the workplace. Links between productive sectors, home and community remain strong. To an extent this compounds the limits to re-negotiating gender and work in the Pacific but more positively may offer the potential for challenging economic and political policies that have been detrimental to Pacific Islands women.

Notes

1 This paper presents initial findings of a team project 'Work, Identity, Ethnicity and Gender in Fiji' led by the author and with postgraduate participants, Sue Carswell and Christy Harrington. Carswell completed fieldwork in a rural canegrowing settlement (1996-7), and is grateful to the FSC and sugar union officials for their assistance. Harrington and Leckie interviewed several respondents in the garment and health sectors. Thanks from Harrington to garment employers who co-operated, and from Leckie to the Ministries of Health and Labour, Public Service Commission. FNZ and the Fiji National Archives generously allowed access to archives. All researchers greatly thank the workers who shared their life stories. The project was assisted by an Otago University Research Grant and affiliation to Development Studies Programme, University of the South Pacific. Special thanks to Cros Walsh, Mele Radrodro, Claire Slatter and Fiji's Department of Women and Culture. The author is responsible for this paper's contents, but gained relevant data and insights from other researchers. Thanks also to comments from two anonymous referees. This is a revised version of a paper presented at the International Conference on Women in the Asia-Pacific Region: Persons, Powers and Politics, Singapore, August 1997.

2   See Amrita Chhachhi and Renée Pittin, 'Multiple Identities, Multiple Strategies' in A. Chhachhi and R. Pittin (eds), *Confronting State, Capital and Patriarchy: Women Organizing in the Process of Industrialization* (Macmillan Press, Institute of Social Studies, Houndmills, 1996), pp. 93-130.

3 Published research on work and gender in the South Pacific was scarce until 'Atu Emberson-Bain (ed.), *Sustainable Development or Malignant Growth? Perspectives of Pacific Island Women* (Marama Publications, Suva, 1994). Earlier publications include, *Special Issue: Women and Work in the South Pacific, Journal of Pacific Studies,* 13 (1987); Caroline Ralston, 'Women Workers in Samoa and Tonga in the Early Twentieth Century', in Clive Moore, Jacqueline Leckie and Doug Munro (eds), *Labour in the South Pacific* (James Cook University of North Queensland, Townsville, 1990), pp. 67-77; Eci Kikau and Penelope Schoeffel, 'Women's Work in Fiji: An Historical Perspective', *Review,* 1:2 (1980), pp. 21-6.

4 Most informants' names have been changed or omitted.

5 Christy Harrington, 'The Empire Has No Clothes? The Experience of Fiji's Garment Workers in Global Context', M.A. Thesis, University of Hawai'i, 1994, pp. 71-6.

6 Caryl Pollard, 'Domestic Service in Suva, Fiji: Socio-economic Factors Affecting Change', PhD Thesis, University of the South Pacific, 1987.

7 Information, Sue Carswell.

8 Harriet Bradley, *Fractured Identities: Changing Patterns of Inequality* (Policy, Cambridge, 1996).

9 See J. Leckie, 'Workers in Colonial Fiji, 1870-1970', in Moore, Leckie and Munro, pp. 47-66.

10 Bureau of Statistics, Annual Employment Survey, provisional report (Suva, 1993).

11 International Labour Organisation/United Nations Development Programme, 'Towards Equality and Protection for Women Workers in the Formal Sector, South East Asia and Pacific Multidisciplinary Advisory Team', draft report (ILO, Suva, 1996), p. 2.

12 See Shaista Shameem, 'Sugar and Spice: Wealth Accumulation and the Labour of Indian Women in Fiji, 1879-1930', PhD Thesis, University of Canterbury, 1990, p. 5.

13 See 'Atu Emberson-Bain, *Labour and Gold in Fiji* (Cambridge University Press, 1994), p. 7.

14 Summarised in Shameem, pp.101-2.

15 *Fiji Times*, 28 July 1960.

16 See A. Haroon Akram-Lodhi 'Structural Adjustment in Fiji Under the Interim Administration', *Contemporary Pacific*, 8:2 (1996), pp. 259-90.

17 David Forsyth, 'Women Workers in Fiji's Formal Sector', unpublished report (University of the South Pacific, Suva, 1996), p. 8.

18 Heather Booth, *Women of Fiji: A Statistical Gender Profile* (Department for Women and Culture, Suva, 1994) provides details.

19 S304/53, Fiji Public Service Association membership sub-committee, 28 April 1978.

20 Provisional data, Management Information Services, Public Service Commission, Suva.

21 Only 196 of 1546 posts are open to promotion, Forsyth, p. 32.

22 Booth, p. 18.

23 Harriet Bradley, *Men's Work, Women's Work: A Sociological History of the Division of Labour in Employment* (Polity, Cambridge, 1989), p. 188.

24 Ibid., pp.193-4, paraphrasing Elaine Showalter.

25 F48/168/1, question in Fiji Legislative Council by B.D. Lakshman, 30 October 1937.

26 GS (general secretary), FNA to Minister, Women's Affairs and Social Welfare, 9 August 1988.

27 See Bradley, *Men's Work, Women's Work*, pp. 169ff.

28 Interview, Emele Naulumatua, 1996.

29 Christy Harrington, 'Impact of Global Restructuring on Women in the Garment Industry' (unpublished paper presented to Women in Politics Conference, UNIFEM, Fiji, 18 November 1996), p. 3. See Kushma Ram, 'Militarism and Market Mania in Fiji' in Emberson-Bain (ed.), *Sustainable Development*, p. 246.

30 Claire Slatter, 'Women Factory Workers in Fiji: The "Half a Loaf" Syndrome', *Journal of Pacific Studies*, 13 (1987), pp. 47-59. There is now extensive global literature on gender stereotypes and global manufacturing since Diane Elson and Ruth Pearson, 'Nimble Fingers Make Cheap Workers: An Analysis of Women's Employment in Third World Export Manufacturing', *Feminist Review*, 7 (1981), pp. 87-107.

31 Roman Grynberg and Kwabena Osei, 'Rules of Origin Disputes and Competitiveness in the Fiji Garment Export Industry' (Economics Department, University of the South Pacific, Suva, 1996), p. 15, cites these employer perceptions. Forsyth reproduces this in his 1996 pilot study, based on statements of nine garment workers. On average, women have lower pay than men in Fiji's public service. Here the rationale is that women, unlike men, have not regarded employment in the civil service as a life-long career. See Jacqueline Leckie, *To Labour with the State: The Fiji Public Service Association* (University of Otago Press, Dunedin, 1997), pp. 82-7.

32 Christy Harrington, *Migration of Garment Workers: A Case Study of Three Suva Factories* (Ministry of Women and the Ministry of Labour, Department of Geography, University of the South Pacific, Suva, 1994), p. 90.

33 See also Emberson-Bain (ed.), *Sustainable Development*.

34 Peggy Fairbairn-Dunlop, 'Mother, Farmer, Trader, Weaver, Juggling Roles in Pacific Agriculture', in Emberson-Bain (ed.), *Sustainable Development*, pp. 73-90.

35 Department for Women and Culture, 'Country Report – Fiji. Review of Implementation of the Nairobi Forward-Looking Strategies for the Advancement of Women, 1985-1992' (Suva, 1995), p. 10.

36 Ibid., p. 5. Four per cent were joint loans.

37 Indigenous Fijians living in villages also face problems of labour supply for subsistence and cash production as there is not always communal reciprocity of labour. The latter is more prevalent in Indo-Fijian farming settlements than is often

acknowledged.
38 Ralston, pp. 74-5.
39 F48/168, draft, Medical Department to Governor General, NZ, 18 June 1936.
40 Legislative Council of Fiji, Council Paper 39/1969.
41 South Pacific Commission, *National Review of the Nairobi Forward-Looking Strategies for the Advancement of Women* (Noumea, 1995).
42 Ganesh Chand, 'The Labour Market and Labour Institutions in Fiji in an Era of Globalisation and Economic Liberalisation' (unpublished paper, Fiji Trades Union Congress, 1996), pp. 28-31, queries official unemployment rates of 10.2 per cent in 1987 and 6 per cent in 1995. His revised figures crudely suggest 10.6 per cent and 19.3 per cent.
43 Shameem, p. 411.
44 F48/168, memo, Director Education and Director Medical Services, 5 March 1936.
45 Department for Women and Culture, p. 24.
46 Ibid., p. 10.
47 International Labour Organisation/United Nations Development Programme, p. 24. Figures from the regional University of the South Pacific. These are not broken down by nationality so the proportion of female students from Fiji is unclear.
48 *Soqosoqo ni Vakavulewa*, a political party headed by coup leader and Prime Minister Rabuka and President Ratu Sir Kamisese Mara.
49 For example, S203/161, Labasa Housing Committee, Fiji Public Service Association to heads of departments, 4 October 1975; *Fiji Times,* 5 February 1982.
50 Central Whitley Council, minutes, 1 April 1977.
51 S221/163, officer to gs, FPSA, 30 Sept. 1982. Forsyth cites a similar recent example, p. iii. See Booth, pp. 18-20, for a statistical breakdown of gender and promotions.
52 *Fiji Times,* 3 October 1990; FNA, Joint Staff Side Paper, 'Victimisation of Nurses' (n.d.)
53 In 1991 Fiji's Poverty Task Force estimated a family of five needed $58.11/week for basic survival. Jenny Bryant *Urban Poverty and the Environment in the South Pacific* (University of New England, Armidale, 1993), p. 75, included those vulnerable to poverty and estimated $72.37/week was necessary for an average household of six in 1991.
54 Ibid.
55 *Fiji Poverty Report* (United Nations Development Programme/Government of Fiji, Suva, 1997), p. 39.
56 Bryant, p. 79, Booth, p. 59, cite Housing Assistance and Relief Trust (HART) figures, showing 80 per cent of very poor families housed by HART have a female head.
57 For example, *Fiji Times*, 27 January 1990.
58 Harrington, anthropology seminar, University of Otago, 1 May 1997.
59 FNA, *Annual Report,* 1995. This percentage does not include student nurses, of whom 43 were union members that year.
60 Viti Registered Nurses' Association (a precursor of FNA), executive meeting, 13 April 1971, raised the issue of nurses at risk.
61 MD 18/2, Divisional Medical Officer, Western to Director Medical Services, 25 May 1959.
62 *Fiji Times*, 26 August 1983.
63 Ethnic composition of the nursing division at 15 March 1996 was 71 per cent Fijian, 26 per cent Indian, 3 per cent others (Ministry of Health).
64 Jacqueline Leckie, 'Industrial Relations in Post-Coup Fiji: a Taste of the 1990s', *New Zealand Journal of Industrial Relations,* 17 (1992), pp. 5-21.
65 *Fiji Times*, 10 October 1990; *Fiji Times*, 2 November 1990.

66 *Fiji Times*, 5 March 1991, quoting striking garment worker.
67 Forsyth, p. 16.
68 These observations are not to denigrate other causes such as nutritional deficiencies, violence, or spirituality, but are examples of the only means women have to negotiate or find space from work.
69 Agricultural Landlords and Tenants Act.
70 Information, Sue Carswell.
71 See Akram-Lodhi, pp. 278-81, for other related constraints

SIX

Deconstructing the 'Exotic' Female Beauty of the Pacific Islands[1]

TAMASAILAU M. SUAALII

'Exotic' images of the Pacific Island woman have long been emblematic of the beauty attributed by foreigners to the islands of the Pacific.[2] Her beautiful body appears in tourist posters and guides, in the pages of such major international journals as the *National Geographic*, in academic texts, on music album covers, on postcards, and in works of fine art, to entice and entrance, to captivate and fascinate. These myriad images are idealised constructions of the female Pacific Island beauty as 'other', as 'body', as 'sexual', as essentially 'exotic'.

This essay is an exploratory deconstruction of the myth of 'exotic' beauty synonymous with Pacific Island women, particularly as it is constructed by 'white' male desire. My use of the label 'white' is a gloss on the rather ambiguous Samoan word papalagi which labels both that which is perceived as European and more broadly that which is viewed as foreign. My usage here refers even more specifically to what social scientists, equally ambiguously, refer to as 'middle-class European'. I want to elucidate the paternalistic, eurocentric, phallic-orientated images which create fields of contested meanings around representations of Pacific Island women, representations opportunistically used by makers of images – writers, artists, photographers – for various ends that, more often than not, appeal to the heterosexual male of white colonial, neo-colonial and 'post-colonial' society.[3]

My focus is on constructions of the exotic female beauty of the Pacific Islands and how these constructions are fed and defined by white consumption and by eurocentric male desires. I examine a series of visual images from several sources to illustrate the production of hidden messages embedded in colonial and post-colonial constructions of the 'exotic'. Another dimension of representations of the female 'exotic' is added by juxtaposing images of the exotic with images of the 'erotic'.

The essay attempts to address the persistence of colonial constructions which serve to demean the status of Pacific Island women. It also seeks to provide insights into the practical and academic significance of deconstructing colonial and post-colonial images of Pacific Island women, and uncovering the complexities of the production of meaning within fixed and lived contexts.

I have not attempted to give an exhaustive account or present an extensive collection of depictions of Pacific Island females, but have sought to trigger thoughts and further discussions about how they have been, and in many cases still are, portrayed. For myself, a Western Samoan woman raised in New Zealand, my questions, experiences and understandings are ultimately set and located within a generation of Pacific Islanders who live and move primarily between two very different social/cultural formations. I locate myself with women with whom I share cultural biographies, and it is from them that I draw much, if not all, of my strength and legitimacy in re-narrating and rewriting the stories of re/presentation and mis/representation experienced by our Pacific Island women.

The Exotic as 'Orientalised Other'

A dictionary definition is a useful starting point in understanding what is meant by the term 'exotic'. The term is described as synonymous with the following words or phrases: 'outside; foreign; … strange or different in a way that is striking or fascinating; strangely beautiful, enticing …'.[4] These terms and concepts are commonly used to describe the *beauty* of the tropical settings of the Pacific Islands, as well as the peoples who dwell therein, the Pacific Islanders themselves.

In understanding the construction and maintenance of the 'exotic' as foreign, outside or other to the West, the theoretical tool of 'Orientalism' developed by Edward Said proves highly useful. This tool can assist in uncovering and explaining the processes and techniques required for the persistent manufacturing of the exotic in contemporary modern societies. Said uses Orientalism to refer to three main things, each of them interdependent. He explains that firstly it may be used in an academic sense:

> The most readily accepted designation for Orientalism is an academic one … Anyone who teaches, writes about, or researches the Orient – and this applies whether the person is an anthropologist, sociologist, historian, or philologist – either in its specific or its general aspects, is an Orientalist, and what he or she does is Orientalism.[5]

Second, it may be used more generally, in a sense that intertwines with the academic:

> [There] is a more general meaning for Orientalism. Orientalism is style of thought based upon an ontological and epistemological distinction made between 'the Orient' and (most of the time) 'the Occident'. The interchange between the academic and the more or less imaginative meanings of Orientalism is a constant one, and since the late eighteenth century there has been a considerable, quite disciplined – perhaps even regulated – traffic between the two.[6]

And third, it may also be used to refer more specifically to corporate institutions (such as tourism) that specifically deal with manufacturing the Orient as exotic:

> Orientalism is something more historically and materially defined than either of the other two .... Taking the eighteenth century as a roughly defined starting point Orientalism can be discussed and analyzed as the corporate institution for dealing with the Orient ... in short, Orientalism, as a Western style for dominating, restructuring, and having authority over the Orient.[7]

Here I focus on this idea of orientalising the exotic to read as other to the West. Seemingly contradictory images of the exotic beauty of the Pacific Islands and their inhabitants as both actively savage and passively sensual are manifested, commodified, and sold by the West to the West, particularly through orientalised images of the exotic *female* beauty of these islands. Such images of exotic female beauty are controlled and maintained by the West for its consumption and pleasure. Such notions of the exotic Pacific Island female locate her as the sensual, sexual, and savage 'other' of Western society. She is simultaneously both outside, foreign, strange, different, striking or fascinating, strangely beautiful, [and] enticing in a way that is both contradictorily 'savage' on the one hand and 'noble' on the other. These seemingly contradictory images of the exotic female beauty as passively 'sensual', and actively 'savage', are selectively re/constructed by the white describer, to fit his orientalised perceptions of the Pacific.

The image of the female beauty of the Pacific Islands as 'different' and 'other' to white patriarchal society is orientalised and manifested in the label 'exotic'. I would contend that the label 'exotic' captures the double marginalisation of women of colour such as Pacific Island women in a way different to the arguments made by white women against/about Western patriarchy. The label 'exotic' is, in this sense, a label which recognises the double 'othering' of Pacific Island women as other to both white males and white females.

The image of the exotic female beauty of the Pacific Islands most commonly found in pages of popular Western fiction, as well as in academic depictions, is that of the 'unmarried' maiden of the South Seas, who has long flowing dark hair covering dusky bare skin, as illustrated in Figure 1 below.[8] The image was found in the pages of the highly circulated *National Geographic* magazine with a caption that read 'Fragrant blossoms cling to the spun-jet tresses of a South Seas maiden, 20 year-old Moira Fabricius of Apia. Her features reflect her mixed ancestry – Chinese, Polynesian, and Danish. She wears blooms over the left ear to signify that she is unmarried'. The model's sensual appeal lies not only in the naturalness of her bare skin covered only by her 'spun-jet tresses', and her suggestive sexual availability symbolised by the phallic 'blooms over her left ear', but also in her 'mixed ancestry' which provide the more 'refined' and colonially pleasing features held and/or sought by white women of the West.[9] The 'refined features' of the 'sensual female exotic' image become obvious

Figure 1   Figure 2

when juxtaposed with the 'exotic female savage' of Micronesia illustrated in Figure 2.[10]

Personifying the exotic within contradictory images of Pacific Island women as sensual and savage has been a process controlled, maintained and targeted to the persistent desires for consumption of exotic female beauty by white males from the so-called sexually repressed societies of Christian Europe in the eighteenth and nineteenth centuries through to the more secular societies of modern Europe.[11] Therefore, in understanding constructions of the 'exotic' as products of the processes of orientalism and consumption, the exotic may be read as demeaning of that which it labels. Images of the savage/sensual exotic are well known to the tourism industry of modern capitalism.

Tourism and the 'Exotic'

The business of tourism plays a central role in the persistence of the exotic in the Pacific Islands. Tourism, argues Tongan writer Konai Helu Thaman, was and continues to be

> a major contributor to, as well as manifestation of, a process of cultural invasion that began in earnest with the spread of Christianity and Western colonial interests in the nineteenth century and has continued more recently, thanks to modern Western technological advancement, to the universalization of Western – mainly Anglo-American market-oriented, capitalist, monetized – culture.[12]

This 'cultural invasion' conducted by the capitalist institution of tourism, manifests itself in the label 'exotic'. The exotic is produced and re-produced by the corporate institutions of tourism and trade to feed off the desires of white males as institutionalised and romanticised in twentieth-century novels such as those by James A. Michener, as well as in the persistent images of the picturesque postcards advertising the Pacific in nineteenth-century Europe.[13] Pierre Rossel, in examining the capitalist institution of tourism and how it manufactures the exotic, locates the orientalised romanticised understanding of the exotic in what he cynically describes as a cultural encounter between tourists and natives. He writes:

> Those who support tourism say that the trips are very enriching in cultural terms: they help to give a better understanding between peoples and cultures. Who believes this? As holidays are an important part of their budget, tourists want 'to get something for their money'; they don't just want to have an interesting time and to lose themselves. They will get what they expect, a setting will be created and a performance given; they will see something of the 'natives'. On their return home they will doubtlessly feel they have discovered a reality of which they were previously unaware.[14]

Rossel confirms Helu Thaman's suggestion that the encounter between the Pacific Islands or the Pacific Islanders and tourism is a constructed and exploitative one that plays on orientalised romanticised understandings of the islands and the islanders as the exotic 'other' of the West. Moreover, Rossel suggests that tourists, as the passively naive agents of corporatised tourism, are largely unaware of their exploitative actions, but instead find their encounters with the exoticism of the Pacific to be, at least for themselves, a culturally enriching experience. It is a perception that exemplifies the subtle techniques of orientalism. Rossel writes that:

> [Tourists] will only have seen what they were intended to see and nothing of the real life of the people. Thanks to the photographs, they will be able to tell their friends that they 'know' the country ... [and its peoples]; meanwhile they have no idea of the implications of their trip.[15]

Here Rossel adds to Helu Thaman's concern that to preserve traditional cultural practices for the sake of the tourist creates fixed understandings of exotic cultures. On the one hand, the conservation of culture for tourism tends to lead to the reification of culture and cultural norms as unchanging and, on the other, it leads to the mystification of culture as exotic. Therefore, preserving culture to the expectations of the tourist ensures the dynamics of some cultures remain static, allowing for the representation of a selective, pseudo-authentic 'culture' to be conserved as 'traditional' – in which the 'exotic' is manifest.

The Pacific tourism industry rests opportunistically on exotic (female) beauty, reflected in the image of the 'orientalised sensual other' as seen in Figures 1 and 3.[16]

Figure 3

The 'sensual exotic' tourist images of Figures 1 and 3 are used not only to sell objects such as sun-tanning products, but also to sell the image of the exotic female as one who is barely clothed, sun-tanned, and with long flowing dark hair. With the 'refined' exotic features of a mixed heritage, and by the symbolic representation of the hibiscus blooms at her ear, she invites and welcomes the tourist viewer to an image of the islands as a place to explore the sensuality of the 'Pacific Island' woman.

Tourism therefore effectively assists in commodifying and perpetuating the orientalised female beauty of the Pacific Islands as the sensual/sexual exotic other of the West, by subversively preserving, homogenising, mystifying – and managing – selective parts of Pacific cultures and cultural practices. In a further commodification, the exotic as the sensual other is capable of being located also as the transgressive 'occult' other of the West.

The Exotic as 'Occult'

To understand notions of the exotic as occult, John C. Gowan's book on the 'exotic' abilities and supernatural powers of 'mankind' proves useful. He describes the abilities of psychics as exotic because of their involvement and possession of occult knowledge and powers. Gowan calls these exotic powers 'strikingly unusual'. He writes: '[c]uriously enough, it is not the magnitude and ability of a [exotic, occult] power which excites admiration and surprise in us, it is the "strikingly unusual" aspect.'[17]

Gowan argues that exotic powers are bestowed from 'above'. One might add, by analogy, that Pacific Island women are also imposed upon in this way. While the analogy may appear far-fetched, I contend that on closer analysis it serves a useful purpose. The analogy not only allows some links to be drawn between orientalised notions of the exotic female as the 'sexual other' of white patriarchal society, but also suggests that the exotic is constructed in other settings as 'something more', something 'occult', something transgressive. Gowan's conception that the occult powers of the psychic are exotic in a 'strikingly unusual' sense, may be extended to a conception of the orientalised beauty of the Pacific Islands as possessing similar mysterious occult powers over her white male viewer.

Gowan's analysis of exotic power invokes images of the occult attributed to western representations of black women who practise 'black magic' or 'voodoo', popularised in American horror films labelled 'exotic thrillers'. Closer to home, it conjures up comparable images, of stories told of Samoan female aitu (god-like demons or ghosts, who are, more often than not, ancestors or recently deceased relatives), who roam at night and punish people for sexual and other misconduct.[18]

The image of the exotic as occult therefore can be linked to images and stories of the knowledge and powers of the aitu, many of whom are women. These exotic powers are believed in by many Pacific peoples, and passed on to successive generations, but are dismissed in the main by Western discourse as domestic fables, myths and legends – not 'real', although interestingly exotic, different. This representation or mis/representation of the exotic as occult necessarily produces the occult as fiction. To present the exotic female beauty of the Pacific Islands as possessing 'strikingly unusual', but 'real' knowledge and powers of the occult would destroy conservative myths of the exotic as the passive and containable savage. Preserving notions of the exotic-as-occult as fiction, rather than non-fiction, provides a context where the viewer has control, where his transgressive fantasies and desires may be fulfilled without having to expose his fear of occult powers that lie outside his control.

The exotic-as-occult not only further perpetuates images of the exotic as mysterious, but also suggests that occult images, although sexually provocative, are fictional and only figments of over-active native imaginations. The fictionalising and orientalising of images of the exotic-as-occult, and as existing only in the minds of the overly spiritual native, is illustrated by the self-depiction of Tokelau artist, Fuimanu Kirifi, as a fictional aitu carrying the burdens of orientalised representations of the Pacific in his painting titled 'Night' in Figure 4.[19]

This painting is returned to later in my discussion of indigenous Pacific Island portrayals of the exotic. It is located here not only to highlight a representation that may be read as the exotic occult, but also to suggest how white viewers may view themes of the exotic-as-occult in the Pacific Island female's interactions with others in the dark images of the night. The connotations of darkness associated with the exotic-as-occult, as night-time realities of native imaginations, may be further extended in examining notions of the exotic as pornographic.

The Exotic as Pornographic

Within notions of the occult runs a theme of transgression that may be similarly found in notions of the female pornographic other of the West. Through this theme, and that of commodification, images of the female exotic may be linked to Western pornographic images of the female erotic.

Figure 4

The naked images of white women, popularised in so-labelled pornographic male magazines such as *Playboy*, publicise and commodify images of women as examples of the sexual other of the West. *Playboy* images (Figures 5 and 6)[20] publicly display the naked female body for the male consumer; these images of the pornographic other are often displayed in a manner not dissimilar to the display of the Pacific Island female body as illustrated in Figures 7 and 8.[21]

The body of the exotic female beauty is often a listless body whose owner seems ambivalent. The Pacific Island woman is often portrayed as staring away from the colonial gaze, in contrast to images of the pornographic other who (in the images above) seems to engage directly with the viewer. The seeming ambivalence of the Pacific Island woman distances her from the viewer in a way that creates and sustains an aura of mystery that serves to simultaneously fascinate and captivate the viewer. Her 'ignorance' of the viewer implies a lack of resistance to being gazed upon. The appeal of her mysterious presence for the viewer is assisted by her partial nakedness, as the viewer is only able to gaze upon part of what makes her 'woman'. In contrast, the pornographic subject is typically photographed not only (directly or indirectly) acknowledging the existence of a viewer, but also as totally exposing her 'womanhood'. Her appeal lies precisely in her blatantly and transgressively exposed body.

The exotic female beauty and the pornographic female beauty 'appeal' to the fantasies and desires of white male consumers in different ways. Nevertheless, there exists a striking similarity in these images. This raises questions about how such similarities work in the minds and fantasies of those who consume them, particularly those who hold positions of power. Analysing the link between the exotic and the pornographic suggests a complex web of domination and self-regulation where the subject – both the pornographic other and the Pacific Island

Figure 5 (*above left*)
Figure 6 (*above right*)
Figure 7 (*right*)
Figure 8 (*below*)

Figure 9

woman – becomes the product for male consumption.)

The commodification of the pornographic might be said to feed much the same market as the 'exotic female' in modern patriarchal societies. However, unlike the seemingly easy transportation of exotic female images across popular, academic, High Art and other ideological boundaries, any like attempt to move images of the 'pornographic female other' has been highly resisted. The commodification of the exotic as similarly pornographic, and its transportability across different ideological and representational domains in modern capitalist societies, is well exemplified in Figure 9.[22]

This image illustrates how a Pacific Island woman is commodified, controlled and orientalised (for the viewer) as 'mystical' body, sexual, exotic. It also shows how the images of Figures 5 and 7 are easily perpetuated in yet another domain for legitimate Western consumption, i.e. the highly competitive and legitimate market of popular music. Such images of the exotic as pornographic, or as occult, have been further used by Pacific Islanders themselves, though for somewhat different ends.

Indigenising the Exotic: 'Parodic Postmodern' Images

Today the 'exotic' may be found in the works of Pacific Island fashion designers and artists in New Zealand, as represented in Figures 4 and 10[23] respectively. Here we have examples of the indigenising of the exotic in the sense that Pacific peoples themselves have taken colonial constructions of the beauty of the Pacific Islands, and redefined and relocated the exotic as an identity that they adopt rather than one that is imposed. The new, 'indigenised exotic' seems to play on what Linda Hutcheon calls 'parodic post-modern representations' of the past into a new understanding of the present. Hutcheon writes that:

> this parodic reprise of the past of art is not nostalgia; it is always critical. It is not ahistorical or de-historicizing; it does not wrest past art from its original historical context and reassemble it into some sort of presentist spectacle. Instead, through a double process of installing and ironizing, a parody signals how present representations come from past ones and what ideological consequences derive from both continuity and difference.[24]

Each of the fashion designs highlighted in Figure 10 co-opt representations of the exotic as sexual while, at the same time, redefining the exotic as

Figure 10

indigenous, mimicking the West's notion of the sensual sexual other in suggestively parodic post-modern representations. The fashion designs indigenise the exotic by using ethnic artefacts such as scallop shells for a bikini bra; by representing the exotic as 'foreign' in the contemporary design of a 'Moon Queen' outfit; by incorporating the lavalava (sarong) worn by (Pacific Island) men as a contemporary statement of the indigenised exotic; and by representing the exotic as the sexual deviant dressed in what is called a 'Tongan bondage' outfit with whip in hand – no longer the passive sexual being depicted in earlier constructions of the exotic. Each of these designs attempt to redefine and represent notions of the exotic in a manner more interactive and engaging than those of the earlier depictions of the exotic as orientalised, occult and passively pornographic. Both the models and the clothing exude an idea of the exotic as engaged/practised rather than as passive object of the colonising gaze.

Fuimanu Kirifi's painting (Figure 4) also presents a play on parodic postmodern representations of the exotic. He highlights the Pacific Island woman in what may appear as settings that mirror those of colonial constructions. However he represents and indigenises the 'exotic' from an insider perspective. His painting depicts Pacific Island images in 'darkness' – the 'darkness' of representations of women, of spirituality, of sexuality. He presents a complex of interacting images emerging from the 'darkness': the sexuality of the couple embracing in the water at the top right-hand corner, the ghost-like image of the artist himself staring right at the viewer in the lower right-hand corner, and the women as parodic representations. The three women depicted in the painting may be read as 'one': the woman at the far left is a representation of the 'exotic' nude woman of High Art; the second rising to stand up is the half-dressed pornographic 'exotic' with gaze averted; and the centred, fully clothed woman reaching towards the little boy in middle-ground is the Pacific woman in context. The artist places the 'sexual' in the background, removed as it is in Christian-defined Pacific sexuality. The representation of 'exotic' women reproduces familiar images but questions their usual meanings, and the three together convey a complex vision of women in Pacific Island societies.

The work by Kirifi acknowledges the blurred boundaries of meaning that surround Pacific Island images. The use of the 'night' to parody the contradictions of Pacific Island female representation is most cleverly done. He draws upon and contests the eurocentric images of the Pacific but also acknowledges their place in Pacific history or herstory. Such parodic representations are made possible in New Zealand's political climate today where issues of biculturalism and multiculturalism are being more publicly debated by its Pacific Island minorities.

Figure 11 (*top*), Figure 12 (*bottom*)

Images in Lived Contexts: De-orientalising the Exotic

The last of my images are of Pacific Island women that exist without the orientalised constructions of the exotic as sensual, savage, or other. They exist as depictions of women in lived contexts. The images of Figures 11 and 12 locate Pacific Island women within their work environment: a Samoan woman at work in a wire factory in Auckland, New Zealand; and a Tongan woman at work preparing to weave a mat, in Tonga.[25] These pictures help to re-contextualise, de-orientalise, and de-exotify images. It is the construction and maintenance of such images of the 'de-exotified' Pacific Island woman in lived contexts that this essay seeks to promote.

Conclusions

Since the disruption of the colonized/colonizer mind-set is necessary for border crossings to not simply reinscribe old patterns, we need strategies for decolonization that aim to change the minds and habits of everyone involved in cultural criticism.[26]

The orientalised linkage of the exotic with the sensual, the savage, the erotic, and the occult, evokes disputed or contrary meanings of the Pacific Island woman as the 'sensual natural native' or the 'shy mysterious temptress' on the one hand, and the 'noble savage' on the other.

Only in deconstructing these myriad images and identifying the techniques of orientalism within colonial constructions, can the demeaning effects of the label 'exotic' be reinscribed in a manner that disrupts the 'colonized/colonizer mindset', and empowers the 'exotified' to construct their/our own contextualised images. This essay has attempted to begin this process of deconstruction towards a re-appropriation of Pacific Islands identities and representations as synonymous with their lived realities.

Notes

1 A version of this paper was delivered at the Twentieth International Pacific Islands Studies Conference held at the University of Hawaii, Manoa Campus, Oahu, on the 6th December 1995. Many people have contributed in different ways to the completion of the various stages of this paper, and for their contribution I am indebted. However I wish to acknowledge in particular the assistance of the following persons. *Faafetai tele lava* (thank you very much) to Rhonda Shaw for her time, energies, and willingness to spend time helping me to edit and revise this paper for the above Conference. *Faafetai tele lava* to Associate Professor Judith Huntsman and Dr Alison Jones for their time, energies and willingness to revise and edit this paper for the purposes of this publication. To Dr Lane West-Newman *faafetai tele lava* for encouraging me to explore the complex issues of cross-cultural (re)presentations, cultural parodies, and the politics of 'naming'. *Faafetai tele lava ia te outou mo lo outou fesoasoani ia te au* (thank you all for your assistance).

2 The category 'Pacific Island' and/or 'Pacific Islanders' is an anomalous category that has been used in New Zealand to refer mainly to peoples from the South Pacific Islands of Samoa, Tonga, Niue, the Cook Islands, Tokelau, and more recently, Fiji. See Cluny Macpherson, 'Pacific Islands Identity and Community' in Spoonley et al. (eds), *Nga Patai – Racism and Ethnic Relations in Aotearoa/New Zealand* (Dunmore Press, Palmerston North, 1996), pp. 124-143. However, I extend this label beyond these six island nations to include other Polynesia and Micronesian islands in the Pacific, including the New Zealand Maori, who have shared a similar history of colonial (re)presentations. It is therefore recognised that though the label attempts to homogenise the various cultures within it, it has value as a general category, if only for the fact that these peoples have shared a similar colonial history of being (re)presented as the 'exotic Pacific Island other' of the Occidentalised colonial nations of the 'West'. (I use the terms 'Occidentalised West' in the sense used by Edward Said in his thesis on *Orientalism* – see footnote 5.)

The myriad images of the 'exotic' beauty of the South Seas or the Pacific Islands overwhelmingly depict images of women. Though there do exist images of the actively savage Pacific Island male beauty as defined by Western discourse, there are few images of a passively sensual Pacific Island male. The author acknowledges this as another area for research.

3 See Julia V. Emberley, *Thresholds of Difference – Feminist Critique, Native Women's Writings, Postcolonial Theory* (University of Toronto Press, Toronto, 1993), for an explication of the political and academic problems associated with the term 'post-colonial'. bell hooks also provides comment on this point in her introduction to her book: bell hooks, *Outlaw Culture – Resisting Representations,* (Routledge, New York/London, 1994), pp. 5-6. In this introduction bell hooks states that 'we do not live in a postcolonial world, because the mind-set of neo-colonialism shapes the

underlying metaphysics of white supremacist capitalist patriarchy'(Ibid., p. 6).

4   Guralnik and Gulralnik, *Webster's New World Dictionary* (Prentice Hall Trade, New York, 1970), p. 192.

5   Edward W. Said, *Orientalism* (Pantheon Books, Random House Inc, and Routledge, 1978), reprinted in Padmini Monia, *Contemporary Postcolonial Theory* (Arnold, London, 1996), p. 21.

6   Ibid.

7   Ibid.

8   Image is located in the *National Geographic Magazine*, Vl 1 (1962), p. 581. Emphasis in the original.

9   See comments made by the author (T.M. Suaalii) in the 'cover story' article by Lloyd Ashton and Nevak Ilolahia, 'Have You Ever Thought About Modelling?' in *Mana Magazine,* 17 (August/September 1997), pp. 18-29, 25-27.

10 Figure 2 is from the *National Geographic* magazine (May 1967), p. 703. The caption associated with this image reads 'Micronesia – the Americanisation of Eden'.

11 I use the terms 'modern Europe' here to refer to the Occidental nations of the West, such as those in Europe proper, as well as countries such as the United States of America, Australia, Canada, New Zealand and so forth.

12 Konai Helu Thaman, 'Beyond Hula, Hotels, and Handicrafts: A Pacific Islander's Perspective of Tourism Development' in *The Contemporary Pacific* (University of Hawaii Press, Spring 1993), p. 104.

13 See James A. Michener, *Tales of the South Pacific* and *Hawaii* (Dymock's Book Arcade, Sydney, 1951). See also examples of postcards in Ann Stephen's book, *Pirating the Pacific, Images of Travel, Trade and Tourism* at fn. 22.

14 Pierre Rossel, 'Tourism and Cultural Minorities: Double Marginalisation and Survival Strategies' in Pierre Rossel (ed.), *Tourism: Manufacturing the Exotic* (International Work Group for Indigenous Affairs [IWGIA], Copenhagen, 1988), pp. 1-20, this reference, p. 2.

15 Ibid.

16 Figure 3 is a typical example of an advertisement found in the American teen magazine titled, *Seventeen* magazine (USA, 1985). The actual magazine held by the author was lost before the publication of this essay but the image is commonly found in popular teen and women's magazines.

17 John C. Gowan, *Operations of Increasing Order and Other Essays on Exotic Factors of Intellect, Unusual Powers and Abilities, etc.* (Privately published by the author, Westlake Village, California, 1980), p. 47.

18 The powers of female aitu (god-like demons) have been personally communicated to me by various family members who believe they have experienced encounters with *aitu*. Also see, Terence Barrow, *Women of Polynesia* (Seven Seas, Wellington, 1967), p. 87-9.

19 This painting was initially seen in the *New Zealand Herald*, 6 October, 1994, section 2. Later I was able to view the original canvas displayed in the home of Associate-Professor Judith Huntsman. I am indebted to Judith for her insights into the work and its artist.

20 *Playboy* is a popular pornographic male magazine distributed and consumed in the West. The image was taken from a *Playboy Magazine* (c. 1972). The actual magazine used by the author has been lost. Therefore images are cited as simply from this magazine at around this year.

21 Figure 7 was found in Terence Barrow, *Women of Polynesia* (Seven Seas, Wellington, 1967). Figure 8 is from Ann Stephen's book, *Pirating the Pacific, Images of Travel,*

Trade and Tourism (Powerhouse Publishing, Australia, 1993).

22 This image was found on the music album cover of the album *Siren Songs of the South Seas: Music of the Tropical Isles – Pepe and her Rarotongans* (Vikings Sevenseas Ltd, New Zealand, c. 1970).

A more recent example is the cover of Annie Crummer's music album titled *Seventh Wave* (Warner Music Company, Australia/New Zealand, 1996). Annie Crummer is a New Zealand-raised and based Cook Island singer, who is well known in the New Zealand music scene. On the cover of this single, Annie Crummer, although not as exposed as the Pacific Island woman in Figure 9, is depicted as having long dark flowing hair, an hibiscus at her ear, and her nudity is strategically covered by tropical foliage typically associated with the Pacific Islands. The image re/created by Annie Crummer (or at least by those responsible for her 'image') on this album cover strikes a similar chord of exoticism to that of Figure 1. Its existence today exemplifies the point made throughout this article that the colonial construct of the 'exotic' beauty is a construct that persists, albeit in different ways.

23 This illustration was found in archives of 'Pacific Sisters Fashion Show – at Opening of Tivaevae Exhibition' (Auckland, New Zealand, December 1995) at the Auckland City Art Gallery.

24 See Linda Hutcheon, 'The Politics of Parody' in *Parodic Post-Modern Representation* (Routledge, London and New York, 1989), pp. 93-117.

25 Figure 11 is from Glenn Jowitt, *Pacific Images – Focus on the Pacific* (1987), p. 16. Figure 12 is from a postcard given to me by the former Tongan lecturer in Education at the University of Auckland, Ms Lita Foliaki.

26 See bell hooks, p. 6.

SEVEN

Reflecting on the Pacific:
Representations of the Pacific and Pacific Island Women in Five Dominant Cinematic Texts

JUDITH VAN TRIGT

This essay examines the representation of the Pacific and Pacific Island women in five dominant cinematic texts. It explores the construction of the Pacific as 'other' in Western discourse and cinematic practice. With reference to particular films, dominant cinema is seen to define the Pacific as remote, savage, a paradise under threat. Pacific Island women are seen to be represented as sexually available, silent, the signifiers of difference. This essay questions the extent to which these representations reflect Western fantasies about the Pacific, rather than what the Pacific might 'really' be, and who Pacific Island women 'really' are. It concludes that 'The Pacific' and 'Pacific Island women' are constructions that reinforce a Western concept of Self: the screen images reflect and reproduce the dominant power relations at work in Western discourse on the Pacific.

The films I have looked at are: *Moana – A Romance of the Golden Age* (1926, silent), *South Pacific* (1958), *Hawaii* (1966), *The Bounty* (1984), and *Rapa Nui* (1994).

Moana (1926) is a slice-of-life account of Moana, a young Samoan man approaching adulthood. The narrative shows the preparations made for the ceremony to celebrate Moana's coming of age: the collection and preparation of food, the tattooing, the dance. There is a sub-plot of a developing romance between Moana and Fa'angase, 'the highest maiden of the village'.

South Pacific (1958) is a film adaptation of the Rodgers and Hammerstein stage musical. It is set on a fictional French Pacific island near the fighting in World War II. Nellie, an American Navy nurse, falls in love with Emile, a French plantation owner, but their romance is complicated by Emile's earlier marriage to a Polynesian woman. At the film's end these complications are resolved. A second romance, between Joe, a Navy lieutenant, and Liat, a Tonkinese native, is less happy: Joe is killed and Liat is married, against her will, to a plantation owner.

Hawaii (1966) is based on James Michener's novel of the same name. It is a dramatisation of early missionary contact with Hawaiians in the 1820s and 1830s. It is a saga of conflict between 'native' and 'Christian' values, depicted through the lives of American missionaries Abner and Jerusha Hale, the Hawaiian Ali'i Nui Malama and her family, and the sealers and traders.

The Bounty (1984) is the third Hollywood version of the April, 1789 mutiny, led by Fletcher Christian against Lieutenant William Bligh, on board the *Bounty*. Unlike earlier productions, which tended to focus on Bligh's pathological cruelty as the reason for the uprising, the 1984 version of the story centres on a psychological struggle between the two main characters, and casts Christian as the troubled hero who forsakes all for his Tahitian love, Mauatua.[1]

Rapa Nui (1994) is set on Easter Island in 1660 – a few decades before European contact. It tells the story of Noro, grandson of the ruling ariki mau, or paramount chief, of the Long Ears tribe, who is chosen to compete against his childhood friend Make, of the Short Ears tribe, in the race for the first manutara egg of the season. The winner of the race earns the right to be the supreme chief of the island, the Birdman. Both Noro and Make are in love with Ramana, a Short Ear woman who is not considered fit to marry Noro. The race turns into a battle for the right to Ramana as well as the status of Birdman.

The Pacific / Pacific Island Women as Other

Edward Said writes that Orientalism as a field of study is a European construction.[2] The Pacific can be likened to the Orient in this manner: it is a Western construct based on generalisations regarding language, race and types. European discourse about the Orient (and, I suggest, the Pacific) is based on establishing the difference between the West and the Rest, between the Self and the inferior Other.[3] Difference from the Western Self is the most salient feature of the Other. The West defines its Self by defining the Other as different, simultaneously denying difference within the category of Other. The Other is conceived of as homogeneous. Establishing difference between Self and Other is crucial: diversity within the category Other threatens the stability of Western Self-identity.[4] Representations of the Other form a system of ascribed meanings, associations and images that become the accepted means of referring to the other in dominant discourse.[5] This system creates a reality which is confused, but does not coincide, with lived experience.[6]

Historically, the West's preoccupation with studying and representing 'Other' cultures has involved clearly differentiating subject from object in ways which support the status quo in terms of power relations.[7] Given the patriarchal nature of Western discourse, it is not surprising that racial and sexual Other-nesses have a tendency to collapse into one, resulting in the sexualisation of non-Western cultures in dominant discourse. The image of the Other is an image of a woman. How women are treated, how they behave and, most importantly, what they look like, signifies the 'truth' of the culture.[8] The dusky maiden signs for the Pacific as a whole and penetration is a metaphor for colonisation: the *Bounty* drops anchor at Matavai Bay – underwater shot of the anchor digging into the sea bed, cut to swarms of bare-breasted Tahitian women swimming out to greet the sailors.

Cinematic practice sets up a particular subject/object relation. Dominant cinema locates the centre/subject position with the spectator, the margin/object position with those who are looked at. The gaze constructs the object/'Other' as separate and different from the subject/'Self', the originator of meaning. Dominant cinema is characterised by a type of address which '[evokes] certain kinds of looking, [advancing] masculine subjectivity as the only subjectivity available'.[9] In viewing the Pacific, dominant cinema invites a kind of looking that is Eurocentric as well as masculine. The gaze defines the Other within the frame, colluding with Western patriarchal power to define the Other within discourse, to produce a visual image of the sexual/racial object that the spectator can recognise and consume.

In viewing the films the questions I considered were: What do these films say about the Pacific and Pacific Island Women and how do they go about saying it? What exchange is there between Western perceptions of the Pacific and Pacific Island women and their representation in dominant cinema? In posing these questions, I recognise that I am perpetuating the construction of the Pacific and Pacific Island women as definable, describable, homogeneous entities. The discussion of these texts assumes an arbitrary, generalising Other-ing of diverse places and peoples. Film-maker Pratibha Parmar writes:

> Images play a crucial role in defining and controlling the political and social power to which both individuals and marginalized groups have access. The deeply ideological nature of imagery determines not only how other people think about us, but how we think about ourselves.[10]

I do not presume to know how the images in these texts affect the ways in which women in Hawaii, Samoa, Tonkin, Tahiti and Easter Island think about themselves. However, by exposing the ideologies at work in Western representations of the Pacific and Pacific Island Women, even as I have relied upon them, I can perhaps explore the ways in which these ideologies and power relations are reproduced in the texts.

Images of the Pacific: Remote, Savage, a Paradise under Threat

The idea of the Pacific as remote makes sense only to a consciousness that resides in the West. Remoteness implies geographic and temporal distance from the point of reference. In cinema, the gaze locates that point of reference as the camera/viewer. In looking, the viewer gains access to the otherwise inaccessible. These films position the viewer as coming from the outside: we make our own journey of discovery in engaging with the text. The opening frames of *Hawaii* and *Rapa Nui* are almost identical: the camera speeds over the ocean towards a distant island. The voice-overs tell us that our destinations are 'that land remote from the rest of the world' *(Hawaii)*, and 'one of the most remote islands on the face of the earth' *(Rapa Nui)*. *South Pacific* and *The Bounty* begin at closer range, with shots of beaches, palm trees, islanders fishing or working in the forest but still at a distance, with the camera positioned slightly off-shore.

All the texts have a historical setting: *Moana* refers to 'the golden age', *South Pacific* is set during World War II, *Hawaii* is set in the third and fourth decades of the nineteenth century, *The Bounty* is set in the late eighteenth century, and *Rapa Nui* in the mid-seventeenth century. The Pacific is depicted as historically apart from the rest of the world, not just behind time, but outside of time. In the introductory stills/voice-overs, a Polynesian history is frequently constructed with reference to the arrival of gods and ancestors. To the Western viewer, this may suggest a history based on fable and myth. The speaker tells us that thousands of years have passed without change until now, until Europeans (and us, as viewers) make, or are about to make, contact *(Hawaii* and *Rapa Nui)*. In *South Pacific*, the opening credits roll over a sequence of shots that begins with a sunrise, continues with glimpses of island life, and concludes with a sunset: this implies that, outside of Western influence, nothing much happens here. The Pacific is portrayed as timeless and changeless.

Savagery in a variety of forms is another marker of the Pacific. Blythe identifies five versions of the Savage in Western discourse: the Noble Savage, the Ignoble Savage, the Romantic Savage, the Comic Savage, and the Dying Savage.[11] In *Moana* the main character is a Noble Savage (athletic, handsome, staunch and impervious to the pain of tattooing); in *Hawaii* it is the Ali'i Nui Malama (powerful, intelligent, wise enough to see the value of Western ways); in *The Bounty* it is King Tynah (royal, intelligent). We see the Ignoble Savage in the Short Ears tribe *(Rapa Nui)*, and the Tofuans/Tongans *(The Bounty)*. The Romantic Savage is personified in Noro and Ramana *(Rapa Nui)*, Liat *(South Pacific)*, Keoki *(Hawaii)*, and Moana *(Moana)*. Crazy Mary in *South Pacific* is the Comic Savage. The Dying Savage is referred to in both *Hawaii* and *Rapa Nui*.

The texts often throw up a contrast between the Noble and the Ignoble Savage. In *Moana* we are told that 'among the islands of Polynesia there is one where the people still retain the spirit and nobility of their great race'. This implies that the people of Savaii are different from all other Polynesians who, presumably, have lost their 'spirit and nobility'. In *Rapa Nui* an identity crisis develops between Noble and Ignoble aspects of the Savage character. Following the destruction of the Long Ears tribe, Make is repelled by his fellow Short Ears who are eating the charred Long Ears remains, saying: 'You can't do this – it's not who we are'. The Noble Savage behaves differently and looks different from the Ignoble Savage. In *Rapa Nui*, the (noble) Long Ears live in an orderly, spacious village and the women wear clothing that covers their breasts. The

Short Ears are dirty and disorganised. They live in a camp of ragged tents where babies cry and animals are on the loose, while the women dance bare-breasted around a fire. In *The Bounty* the (noble) light-skinned, fine-featured, long-haired Tahitians are contrasted with the (ignoble) darker-skinned, round-featured, frizzy-haired Tofuans/Tongans. Nobility is thus defined as coincident with European norms, behaviours and values. Difference within the Other is allowed only as it serves to reinforce the superiority of the Western Self.

Western representations of the Pacific as Savage have a pseudo-anthropological tone. These texts combine appropriately recognisable visual images of the Savage with historical references to suggest that the Pacific represents a history of the species, a childhood of mankind. The Pacific is presented, with a kind of nostalgia, as an example of the simple, natural life of which 'we' were all once a part. At the same time, the Savage clearly denotes difference from the Western, civilised subject, who, these references suggest, is the more highly evolved form of the species.

The third image of the Pacific in the texts is of a Paradise under Threat. Western representational and literary histories are full of visions of the Pacific as terrestrial paradise.[12] This is captured well on film: lush forests, waving palms, golden sands and sparkling seas compare favourably with images of the hardships encountered on sea voyages in the eighteenth and nineteenth centuries. But there is always trouble in Paradise. In *Moana* there is the tyranny of tradition – the tattoo – 'a pattern of the flesh, to you perhaps no more than a cruel, useless ornament [through which] the Samoan wins the dignity, the character and fibre which keeps his race alive'. In *South Pacific* there is the threat of war. In *Hawaii*, traditional and Christian values clash, and Western diseases and economic exploitation threaten the well-being of the Islanders. In *The Bounty* we see the conflict between Christian and Bligh that leads to the mutiny. In *Rapa Nui*, there is class warfare and destruction of the natural environment.

No paradise is complete without a maiden, and in these texts this is, perhaps, where the greatest threat lies. Classic Hollywood narrative poses 'woman as problem', with closure resulting in recuperation of the woman into a proper male/female bond.[13] Romance, typically troubled, is what drives the plot in these movies. In *Moana* there is the burgeoning relationship between Moana and Fa'angase. In *South Pacific* there are two romances: one between Nellie and Emile, the other between Joe and Liat. In *Hawaii* there is the socially sanctioned but passionless marriage between missionaries Abner and Jerusha Hale, a repressed romance between Jerusha and ship's captain Rafer Hoxworth, the abiding but incestuous love between Malama and Kololo, and the traditional, again incestuous, alliance between Malama's son and daughter, Keoki and Noelani. In *The Bounty*, Fletcher Christian's love relationship with Mauatua is seen to be a principal cause of the mutiny. In *Rapa Nui*, the ultimate prize Noro and Make compete for is Ramana, the woman they both love.

Images of Pacific Island Women: Sexual Availability, Silence, Difference

Pacific Island Women in these texts are primarily characterised in terms of their sexual availability. The motif that codes for this is the bare-breasted woman. For the West bare breasts signify female sexuality on display. Bare breasts, fragmented from the rest of the body, are a soft-porn staple.[14] However, not all breasts are relevant: only young, pert, full breasts. Malama *(Hawaii),* and Crazy Mary *(South Pacific),* are always well covered. Cast in what bell hooks calls the 'mammy' role, they are not sexually desirable or available and so they get to keep their tops on.[15] The West's expectation that bare-breastedness is a Pacific cultural norm legitimises the display of women for the pleasure of the masculine spectator. In reality, the celluloid image is not sexually available to the spectator: access is gained by positioning the gaze with the male protagonist to whom the women are available. In *Rapa Nui,* our first glimpse of Ramana, Noro's love interest, is in the village of the Short Ears. It is night, the soundtrack features singing and beating drums as Noro approaches the village.

MCS[16] to CU: Ramana dancing, she looks OS
ELS: Noro comes out from where he is hiding behind a moai
CU: Ramana looks OS towards him, then looks away, then looks back
ELS: Noro runs away
CU: Ramana walks OS
MCS: Fellow villagers watch Ramana leave
LS: Ramana walks away from the village, to moai that we can see Noro hiding behind – Noro grabs Ramana – they embrace and kiss – camera zooms in – Noro and Ramana run OS.

Having introduced Ramana from her lover's point of view, the gaze establishes her as directly accessible for the enjoyment of the spectator. Noro and Ramana run off to be alone. This involves a close up of Noro lying on top of Ramana; both are naked from the waist up. As the camera pans from left to right to concentrate on either Noro or Ramana, Ramana's erect nipples glide from screen left to screen right, always maintaining a prominent position.

In *The Bounty* Mauatua, Fletcher's romantic partner, is also introduced in the context of a village dance. In this example it is a ceremonial dance performed at the planting out of the breadfruit. The dance, we are told, simulates the coupling of men and women, encouraging the gods to do the same so that the harvest will be plentiful. A context of sexual abandon has been created, and it is here that we first see Mauatua, among the crowd that has gathered to watch the dancers.

LS: a woman dancing straddles a man
MCS: Christian watches dancer, then looks OS, as if he feels himself being watched
MCS: Mauatua looks OS, toward Christian, swaying her body from side to side in time to the drum beat

CU:	Christian looks OS toward Mauatua, then in the other direction, as if to verify that she is looking at him
CU:	Mauatua smiles
CU:	Christian smiles, then glances sideways quickly toward
CU:	Bligh, looks from Christian (OS), to Mauatua (OS)
CU:	Mauatua smiles and looks away

These scenes present Ramana and Mauatua primarily in terms of their sexual availability to men, allowing the spectator-voyeur to establish a private relation to them. The 'come-on' look (as in the MCS of Mauatua, above), suggests that the woman is deliberately displaying her body for the spectator, soliciting the gaze.[17] This absolves the spectator from any guilt he may feel in consuming her as a sexual object. The pleasure of the spectator-voyeur is enhanced by the transgressive nature of the sexuality ostensibly on offer (suggested above by the sideways glance toward Bligh, who represents authority and the establishment).

Cinema has a history of defining Black (Other) women's sexuality in terms of transgressiveness and promiscuity.[18] Caroline Ralston identifies the preponderance of sexual images in European depictions of Hawaiian women.[19] Ralston states that 'eroticism and appreciation of sexuality [were] basic motifs of Hawaiian civilization', and therefore Western moralism renders 'prostitution' an inaccurate characterisation of sexual relations between Hawaiian women and European men in the early post-contact period.[20] *Hawaii* exploits this collision of values by presenting Hawaiian women as simultaneously active in soliciting sexual advances, and passive, both in their reception of the (unseen) spectator's gaze, and in terms of narrative action as a whole.

Western discourse on the Pacific silences Pacific Island Women, making them peripheral to history.[21] In cinema 'women do not tell their own stories or control their own images ... the voice of woman ... is systematically absent or repressed'.[22] In *Moana*, Fa'angase symbolises Moana's coming of age; in *The Bounty*, Mauatua represents Christian's resistance to the established order; in *South Pacific*, Liat stands for Joe's longing for 'action' in the Pacific; and in *Rapa Nui*, Ramana is the trophy Noro wins for his achievements. The female characters are relevant only as symbols of the development of the male characters. In some cases the women are literally silenced: Ramana is shut in a cave for half the movie, Mauatua and Liat cannot speak English, and therefore have no lines. An ironic outcome of this situation is revealed in *South Pacific*, when Joe and Liat's relationship is sanctioned by Liat's mother, Crazy Mary. Crazy Mary sings 'Happy Talk': Liat waves her hands, bats her eyelashes and tilts her head, but cannot actually give voice to 'talk about the things [she'd] like to do'.

Non-'mammy', non-sex-object Pacific Island Women are silenced by their absence. There are no sisters, no aunties: the female characters are isolated from any relationships that could link them as individuals to a context other than their definition as symbols in the masculine order.

Pacific Island women are the signifiers of Difference, the embodiment of the Other in these texts. Their sexual availability and silence emphasise the way in which they are different from the European characters on screen. In depicting Pacific women primarily in terms of their sexual relationships with men, sexual difference is privileged above other differences, for example, class. In *Hawaii*, Noelani, the daughter of the ali'i nui, is identified as a member of the chiefly class only by her sexual unavailability to the sailors: this differentiates her from the (commoner) 'co-operative ones'.

Pacific Island women also connote difference in relation to European women in these texts. This relation is characterised by a tension between sisterhood and opposition. In *Hawaii*, Malama embraces Jerusha as her 'adorable little haole sister'. Their friendship is portrayed as warm and affectionate, in contrast with the stormy relations between American and Hawaiian men as they struggle for power. This is an example of dominant cinema's tendency to treat women as a natural grouping, with female characters differing only as to where they fit on the virgin-mother/mammy-temptress-whore role continuum. This Eurocentric notion of sexual difference is then applied cross-culturally.[23] Patriarchal relations of domination are universalised: in the example above, this completely ignores the relative status of Jerusha and Malama in their own cultures.

On the other hand, Jerusha is constructed as the opposite of Hawaiian women. Physically, Jerusha and Malama are opposites: Jerusha is white and petite, Malama is brown and large; Jerusha is servile and industrious, Malama is authoritarian, and in control of an entourage of helpers to meet her every need. Jerusha is the virtuous Christian wife who works tirelessly in the interests of her family and church, in contrast to the Hawaiian women who show no inclination towards housework and the moral life.

Finally, Pacific Island woman as the signifier of Difference is worked over in these texts in the context of the problematic interracial romance. In *South Pacific*, a series of romances – between American Nellie and French Emile (who has had a previous romance with a Polynesian woman), between American Joe and Tonkinese Liat, between Joe and his 'girl' back in Philadelphia – establishes a racial hierarchy that problematises these (d)alliances. When Nellie discovers Emile's former marriage to a Polynesian woman with whom he had children – she has just assumed that the 'native' children playing outside belong to the Polynesian gardener – she has doubts about continuing their relationship.

Nellie gets sympathy from Joe, who is having his own troubles with Liat. They join to sing 'People Like Us', involving the audience in their affirmation of racial segregation, before Joe recants, pointing out that 'You've Got To Be Taught To Hate'. Eventually Nellie's situation is resolved and she moves in to play Mother to Emile's children. Unfortunately Joe dies, and Liat is married off to a plantation owner.

Underscoring the emotional difficulties for the individuals involved in these romances is the threat they pose to the status quo. In *The Bounty* and *Hawaii* we see examples of European men transgressing the boundaries between 'us' and 'them' by 'going native'. It is Fletcher Christian's relationship with Mauatua, and one missionary's marriage to a Hawaiian woman, that symbolises their break with the established order.

Realism and Authenticity

The last issue I want to consider is the extent to which the representation of the Pacific and Pacific Island Women in these texts is 'realistic'. My findings here are in no way authoritative: they are based on my relatively limited research on this point, and the texts I consulted are almost exclusively written by Europeans (and some of these sources are quite old). The five films I looked at involve (at least) five different islands and (at least) six different cultures. This highlights the arbitrary nature of my grouping the films as examples of dominant cinema's treatment of the Pacific. In considering issues of authenticity in these texts, I am not making a final judgement on the accuracy of the representations: rather, I am questioning how spectators come to see a particular representation as 'realistic'.

Film draws on the recording potential of photography, creating the illusion that it captures the world as it really is. Dominant cinema, of which these five films are all examples, is characterised by production processes (for example, continuity editing and the identification of character with narrative development) that are rendered invisible in the final product, giving the illusion that film equals reality.[24] Each of these five texts has real-time, real-place and, in some cases, real-person referents.

Moana opens with a description of the circumstances in which it was made. Robert and Frances Flaherty state that they lived on the island of Savaii for two years, enlisting the help of Fialelei, the chief's granddaughter, as an interpreter between the villagers and themselves. I cannot say how true to life this drama is, and I do not know if the characters were 'real' people.[25]

South Pacific has a real-time referent in being set during World War II. The filming, for the most part, took place on Kaua'i.[26] The narrative is located on an island 'somewhere' in the Pacific. Reference is made to Polynesian 'natives', but a large number of the characters on the island of 'Bali Hai' are said to be Tonkinese.[27]

A.R. Tippett condemns James Michener's novel *Hawaii,* which he says left him 'shocked as an ethnohistorian, appalled as a human being, and completely disturbed that a novel could be so believed at the point of its departure from historicity'.[28] Tippett is most critical of the novel's use (which the film replicates) of real places, times and characters: Laha'ina in the 1820s and 1830s, the New England missionary representatives of the American Board of Commissioners for Foreign Missions.

The Bounty is based on a real-life event. The narrative reveals a number of inaccuracies. In the movie the mutineers return directly to Tahiti; in reality they spent several months at Tubuai before returning to Tahiti twice to collect women and provisions.[29] In terms of the narrative, this would have weakened the contention that Christian is so strongly motivated by his love for Mauatua. In the film, the women leave Tahiti willingly (again, motivated by their feelings for the mutineers). Hough states that a number of Tahitian men and women were duped into staying on board and became aware of their predicament only once the *Bounty* was out to sea.[30] The film also suggests uncertainty about Fletcher Christian's ultimate fate: Hough states that Christian was killed by men he had brought with him from Tahiti and Tubuai, on 20 September 1797.[31] Around the time of its release, much was made of *The Bounty*'s 'authenticity' – a ship had been specially built that was an exact replica of the original *Bounty*. In this instance, authenticity became an issue of prop rather than narrative: 'What actually happened was subordinated to what it would have looked like if it had happened'.[32]

Rapa Nui is clearly a fictional narrative, but it relies on references to history and culture to sustain the drama. The literature confirms the islanders' belief in the settling of Easter Island by Hotu Matua, the existence of a Birdman cult and the race to Motunui for the first manutara egg of the season, the construction and transport of the Moai, and the destruction of the Long Ears by the Short Ears in inter-tribal warfare.[33] The character Ramana's seclusion in the Cave of the White Virgins has historical precedent, according to Heyerdahl, in the sequestering of specially chosen virgins (neru) in a deep cave so that they might become as pale as possible for their role in religious festivals.[34] Wolff claims that young men and women were routinely secluded prior to puberty, when girls would be examined by a priest to certify their virginity (as happens to Ramana in the movie).[35] Heyerdahl states that the responsibility of feeding and caring for youngsters in seclusion fell to women specifically appointed to the task, whereas in *Rapa Nui* Ramana is visited and fed by her competing love interests, Noro and Make.[36]

These texts are, however, dramatic productions and make no stronger claims to historicity than being 'based' on real events. We should not, perhaps, expect that these dramatisations replicate historical events and details. Yet the real-life-like allusions made in historically-based narratives, in conjunction with the realism implied by dominant cinema, create an appetite for authenticity in the audience. Tippett states that many young Americans believe that *Hawaii* (the novel) is 'basically true'.[37] Dening points out that some critics declared the 1962 and 1984 versions of *The Bounty* to be 'unhistorical', for omitting many of the details invented in the 1935 production.[38]

History is produced in culture: culture is not outside history. 'The Pacific' and 'Pacific Island women', as they are represented by these texts, are historically and culturally specific constructions, as are all histories, cultures and representations. Tippett attributes the acceptability of the representation of missionary activity in the novel *Hawaii* to the 'mood of American anti-puritanism and permissiveness that... characterized the fiction of the country in the sixties'.[39] One critic identified a nineties 'greenie' message of protecting the environment in *Rapa Nui*.[40] While the earlier movies considered here [*Moana* (1926), and *South Pacific* (1958)] show no bare-breasted women, the later films feature increasing amounts of nudity.

These texts, then, reflect the norms and expectations of the culture and period in which they are produced. This returns us to the discursive drive, discussed above, to create images of the Other (and consequently the Self) that the audience recognises. Self-representation in the Pacific, and by Pacific Island women, would probably look very different (but would be no less historically and culturally specific). What is at issue here are the relations of power through which dominant discourses name and appropriate the Other for their own consumption. These texts are produced within, and reproduce, these discourses and power relations.

This essay has examined the representation of the Pacific and Pacific Island women in five dominant cinematic texts. The Pacific has been seen to be represented as remote, savage, a paradise under threat. Pacific women have been seen to be represented as sexually available, silent, the signifiers of difference. These representations can in no way be said to reflect the 'real' Pacific, or 'real' Pacific Island women: these categories are themselves arbitrary. Rather, these images reflect a Western construction of the Pacific and Pacific Women as Other, a construction that rests on establishing Difference between Other and Self. In representing the Other, these texts reflect the Self, while emphasising Difference.

The extent to which these representations are accepted as authentic by the predominantly Western audience for which they were created is a condition of the processes of dominant cinematic production, and the historically and culturally specific context in which they were produced.

Notes

1   Greg Dening, *Mr Bligh's Bad Language: Passion, Power and Theatre on the Bounty* (Cambridge University Press, Cambridge, 1992), p. 352.

2   Edward Said, 'from Orientalism', in Antony Easthope and Kate McGowan (eds), *A Critical and Cultural Theory Reader* (Allen and Unwin, Sydney, 1992), p. 63.

3   Ibid., pp. 60-2.

4   Trinh T. Minh-ha, *Woman, Native, Other* (Indiana University Press Bloomington, 1989), p. 98.

5   Said, p. 60.

6   Trinh, p. 94.

7   bell hooks, *Black Looks: Race and Representation* (South End Press, Boston, 1992).

8   Joanna de Groot, '"Sex" and "Race": The Construction of Language and Image in the Nineteenth Century', in Susan Mendus and Jane Rendall (eds), *Sexuality and Subordination* (Routledge, London and New York, 1989), pp. 100-5.

9   Annette Kuhn, *Women's Pictures: Feminism and Cinema* (Routledge and Kegan Paul, London, 1982), p. 63.

10 Pratibha Parmar, cited in hooks, p. 5.

11 Martin Blythe, *Naming The Other: Images of the Maori in New Zealand Film and Television* (Scarecrow Press, Metuchen, N.J. and London, 1994), p. 24.

12 Bernard Smith, *European Vision and the South Pacific 1768–1850: A Study in the History of Art and Ideas* (Oxford University Press, London, 1960), p. 249.

13 Kuhn, *Women's Pictures*, pp. 34-5.

14 Annette Kuhn, *The Power of the Image: Essays on Representation and Sexuality* (Routledge and Kegan Paul, London, 1985), p. 36.

15 hooks, p. 74.

16 The following abbreviations are used: CU=close up, MCS=medium close shot, LS=long shot, ELS=extreme long shot, OS=off screen.

17 Kuhn, *The Power of the Image,* p. 43.

18 Felly Nkweto Simmonds, 'She's Gotta Have It: the Representation of Black Female Sexuality on Film', in Frances Bonner, Lizbeth Goodman, Richard Allen, Linda Janes and Catherine King (eds), *Imagining Women: Cultural Representations and Gender* (Polity Press, Cambridge and Oxford, 1992), p. 220.

19 Caroline Ralston, 'Changes in the Lives of Ordinary Women in Early Post-Contact Hawaii', in Margaret Jolly and Martha Macintyre (eds), *Family and Gender in the Pacific: Domestic Contradictions and the Colonial Impact* (Cambridge University Press, Cambridge, 1989), p. 54.

20 Ibid., p. 57.

21 Sharon Tiffany, in Denise O'Brien and Sharon Tiffany (eds), *Rethinking Women's Roles: Perspectives From the Pacific* (University of California Press, Berkeley, 1984), p. 3.

22 Kuhn, *Women's Pictures*, p. 88.

23 Chandra Mohanty, 'Under Western Eyes: Feminist Scholarship and Colonial Discourse', *Feminist Review*, 30 (1988), p. 64.

24 Kuhn, *Women's Pictures*, p. 38.

25 I have heard that one version of *Moana* ends with Moana and Fa'angase kissing and retiring together to a building on the foreshore, suggesting a romantic resolution. In reality, that building was an outhouse. This scene did not appear in the print I saw.

26 Robert C. Schmitt, *Hawaii in the Movies 1898-1959* (Hawaiian Historical Society, Honolulu, 1988), p. 73.

27 This 'lumping' together of diverse peoples and places illustrates the erasure of difference within Other. Ethnic, cultural and geographic specificities are rendered null as Other is constructed as homogeneously different only in relation to Western Self.

28 A.R. Tippett, *Aspects of Pacific Ethnohistory* (William Carey Library, California, 1973), p. 172.

29 Richard Hough, *Captain Bligh and Mr Christian: The Men and The Mutiny* (Readers Union, 1973), p. 194.

30 Ibid., p. 204.

31 Ibid., pp. 256, 307.

32 Dening, p. 194.

33 Thor Heyerdahl, *Aku-Aku: The Secret of Easter Island* (Allen and Unwin, London, 1958), pp. 43, 124, 145-151; Alfred Metraux, *Easter Island: A Stone Age Civilization of the Pacific* (Andre Deutsch Limited, London, 1957), p. 34: Werner Wolff, *Island of Death: A New Key to Easter Island's Culture through an Ethno-Psychological Study* (J.J. Augustin, New York, 1948), pp. 14-15.

34 Ibid., p. 74.

35 Wolff, p. 24.

36 Heyerdahl, p. 74.

37 Tippett, p. 171.

38 Dening, p. 348.

39 Tippett, p. 172.

40 J. Chilwell, 'Rapa Nui', *Listener,* 21 May 1994, p. 50.

EIGHT

Poems

KONAI HELU THAMAN

Pacific Woman[1]

women produce
reproduce
but cannot choose

how can you call yourself 'free'
when you do not own your body
when you do not decide
whether to get pregnant (or not)

woman
you get up
with the dawn
you walk miles looking
for food
searching for wood
you return bent
with a child
riding on your back
weighing you down

you go alone
to give birth
because you
are unclean
yet your milk
makes them strong
the pig's flesh
is sweet
yet you do not
have a share

you pay
for your right
to keep your place
in their line
with sexual favours
cast out
of your natal home
you are a part-timer
in a new clan
you cannot look back

you must bear children
in-laws watch
your waistline
for the sign
of fulfilment
of their dreams
if you fail
you will suffer
the judgement
of others

woman
you are not
a breeding machine
or a passive pawn
in a man's game
motherhood
does not have
to be an accident
or home economics
or isolation

you are person
you are worker
you are mother
you are woman

Letter to Feifafa

(on the origin of the Kava)[2]

dear feifafa
i have your picture
on my wall
just above
the light switch

your face
is a mixture
of joy and sadness
weaving hope and anxiety
into a royal garland
a story line traces
our origins
among bitter sweet messages
of old

it hurts me
to remember
how she went to be offered
back to the land
how you helped her
to live and die
how you tried to see
her beauty in death
green radiance
of a forgettable dawn

how many times
have you died
from tattooed hands
that torture
and countless unseen wounds
opening through nodes
that connect our sorrows
to the harsh strokes
of society

tear-stained tapa
soaked in blood
continue to flow
from the over-filled kava bowl
of our rulers
their quick acceptance
of your sacrifice
still bleeding
at the cutting edge
of time

i have been thinking
over what you did
that dark day long ago
i still don't believe
that a king was worth it.

Notes

1   First published in Konai Helu Thaman, *Hingano* (Mana Publications, Suva, 1987).
2   First published in Konai Helu Thaman, *Kakala* (Mana Publications, Suva, 1993).
    This poem is about the story (Tongan version) of the origin of the kava plant, which
    was allegedly found by the parents of a young maiden at her gravesite (where her
    head was). She had been killed as a presentation to a young Tongan nobleman (or
    king) because the couple were poor. At her feet grew a sweet tasting plant (sugarcane).
    Today, formal presentations of giant kava plants are always accompanied by mature
    sticks of sugarcane.

NINE

Reclamation of Cultural Identity for Māori Women:
A Response to 'Prisonisation'

D. HELENE CONNOR

This essay is based on my Master's thesis, 'The Resurgence of Mana wāhine: A Response to "Prisonisation": Histories, Reflections and Stories'.[1] In this thesis I explored the notion of 'prisonisation' with reference to Māori women and argued that the reclamation of our cultural identity as Māori or more specifically, our mana wāhine Māori, is one way we can challenge the social consequences of both literal and metaphorical imprisonment.

Essentially, this work looked at the impact of colonisation on Māori identity, a theme which has been extensively researched by a number of influential Māori scholars to whom I am greatly indebted. These scholars include: Graham Hingangaroa Smith, Linda Tuhiwai Smith, Leonie Pihama, Kuni Jenkins, Ngahuia Te Awekotuku, Kathie Irwin and Rose Pere. My research built upon the work of these scholars by looking at the 'imprisonment' of Māori (both literally and metaphorically) and using the themes of identity, race and gender as a type of theoretical filter through which to analyse the narratives of three women.

The idea for the thesis was conceived when I began speculating about a possible connection between the erosion of Māori identity and the high rates of imprisonment for Māori. If there was a connection, I realised it would be difficult to substantiate. Nevertheless I was compelled to develop this hypothesis. I then began to reflect on what I termed metaphorical prisonisation which added another layer of complexity to the project. I surmised that the processes of colonisation had enormous consequences in terms of personal identity for many Māori. Alienation from our land and culture, and being subjected to a process of legal imperialism had ultimately served to imprison Māori identity within an alien Anglo-Celtic culture and political and legal system. Such a scenario had a major effect on both Māori men and women. However, I decided to focus on Māori women because there is a dearth of research for Māori women by Māori women.

This article takes some of the key sections from the thesis and forms a paper divided into five segments. Firstly, an explanation of the concept of prisonisation is given, followed by an historical overview of the European view of 'ideal' womanhood and how this view impacted upon Māori women. A discussion of

Māori identity follows this segment and then fragments of stories of three Māori women ex-prisoners are told in order to humanise and give a voice to the statistics which show that over 50 per cent of all women in New Zealand prisons are Māori. The article concludes with a discussion of the impact of mana wāhine in the context of lives reclaimed.

Prisonisation

Prisonisation is a concept that implies incarceration both within a penal institution and beyond the prison walls. In the metaphorical sense, prisonisation refers to the process of colonisation whereby Māori became 'captives' of British cultural imperialism. In the literal sense, prisonisation refers to the high levels of actual incarceration in penal institutions for Māori. Imprisonment rates for women in Aotearoa/New Zealand are relatively low in comparison to men, nevertheless, census figures for women in prison demonstrate that Māori are disproportionately represented. On 12 August 1994, there were 223 women in New Zealand prisons and, of these women, 114 identified as Māori. The most recent Prison Census carried out on 23 November 1995 stated that of the 140 sentenced women who answered the question of ethnicity, seventy eight identified as Māori and of the thirteen women in remand, eleven of these identified as Māori.[2]

Historically, the Treaty of Waitangi, signed between the British and Māori in 1840, signalled the metaphorical imprisonment of Māori. The introduction of a British legal system eroded Māori systems of justice and social control and enabled the colonisers to acquire Māori land. Policies of amalgamation and assimilation eroded Māori mana, culture and identity, while Christianisation served to heathenise Māori spirituality. Historically, these processes impacted on all Māori. However, men and women were ultimately affected in different ways. Māori women were subjected to a restructuring process which eroded their mana in far more insidious ways. Prior to European contact, Māori women's status and role in society was determined by the hierarchical structures of the iwi, hapu and whānau. Highborn women, for example, could own land and would not lose it upon marriage. With colonisation, the European concepts of 'ideal' womanhood were transferred to Aotearoa and applied to Māori women.

European Models of 'Ideal Womanhood' and Their Application to Māori Women

The creation story of Eve and later the Catholic dichotomy of the two Marys, the Virgin Mary and Mary Magdalene, had a powerful and complex effect upon models of 'ideal' womanhood influencing European colonisers. Eve, the original woman in Judaeo Christian accounts of creation, was constructed as both corrupting and corruptible. She was seen as a wilful temptress who lacked self control over her appetites and passions and was morally inferior to Adam. These commonly held patriarchal and misogynist interpretations of Eve served to form what Rosemary Radford Ruether has termed a theology of subordination which positioned men as being superior to women and viewed a patriarchal social order as being divinely created and natural.[3] Under a theology of subordination, women in Christian Europe had to be kept under the control of men lest they subvert male virtue and rationality. The theology of subordination also constructed women as intellectually and morally inferior to men and created a model of ideal womanhood and femininity for women to aspire to. This carefully contrived ideal was modelled on the Virgin Mary, mother of Jesus and Queen of Heaven; she was the ultimate paragon. Mary stood for piety, subservience and goodness, whereas Eve and also Mary Magdalene represented the fallen woman, fallen from innocence, corrupt and corrupting. The Virgin Mary was the epitome of maternal love and charity. Yet for all her virtues, the Church did not hesitate to stress the subordinate role of Mary to Jesus, nor was worship of her to detract from the dignity and efficacy of Christ. The ideal model of femininity was thus highly ambivalent. Women could strive to emulate Mary with all her worthy virtues, yet they would always remain inferior and subordinate to men just as Mary remained inferior and subordinate to Jesus.

Although models of 'ideal womanhood' may not have used the terms Virgin Mary and Mary Magdalene, stereotypes of 'good' and 'bad' women endured, and women were described in terms of their sexuality. Examples include: virgins and whores, maidens and sluts, God's police and damned whores (to borrow Anne Summer's phrase[4]). Women either conformed to the Virgin Mary's pious form or they 'fell' to Mary Magdalene's depths of depravity and degradation.

Societal definitions of European women thus rested on a dichotomy which arguably bore little relation to the reality of women's lives at any level of social stratification. Although these stereotypes were challenged, there could be no equality between the sexes under a system of patriarchy where male domination was expressed through the power of the State, the family and the Church. The ideals of femininity cast women, particularly middle-class women, in the role of wife, mother and protector of moral values. The ideal woman was supposed to be submissive, modest, quiet, altruistic, self-sacrificing, patient, pure and caring. She was to be schooled in household management and etiquette and was to create a domestic paradise for her husband and children. She was to be an 'Angel in the House'.

Canons of feminine conduct reinforced such a role. One manual, entitled *The Women of England, their Social Duties and Domestic Habits,* authored by Mrs Sarah Stickney Ellis,[5] was basically a guide for women which defined their role as preservers of the home and the 'moral fibre of the nation'. This manual was published in 1839, prior to the first substantial group of settlers leaving England destined for Aotearoa and one can only speculate how many of the migrant women read Mrs Ellis's guide to feminine 'social duties'. It is probable that a number of women were influenced to some degree by the attitudes expressed in this and similar 'advice' books. It is also probable that both men and women internalised such beliefs about women's role and place in society and accepted the stereotypes that women either conformed to the Virgin Mary or the Mary Magdalene prototype and, consciously or not, brought these ideologies with them; ideologies that would ultimately define indigenous women from a Pākehā perspective.

How European models of 'ideal womanhood' were applied to Māori women is difficult to ascertain. It is feasible to surmise that we were compared with European models of 'ideal' womanhood and subsequently judged as conforming to the Mary Magdalene prototype. Eroticised in the journals of the European explorers of the Pacific, Polynesian and Māori women were constructed as dusky skinned, South Seas maidens, amorous, exotic, sensual and sexually available. From a Pākehā position, the commercial exploitation of Māori women as prostitutes for the early European sailors automatically rendered them a pariah class, the fallen woman, contaminated by sin and degradation. From a Māori perspective, however, Māori women would only have engaged in sexual exchanges with Pākehā men if there was something to gain for the benefit of the collective hapu and iwi.

Māori women were not only constructed in terms oppositional to the ideal of European womanhood; the construction of Māori femininity by Europeans was also subject to racism. We were often defined in less than human terms; dehumanised through a process of metaphorical language and likened to animals. As Linda Tuhiwai Smith states:

> Hierarchies of race were used not only to position us as indigenous people in relation to white, Anglo-Saxon British stock, but also in relation to other indigenous people, to the animal world ...[6]

Within the context of colonisation, theories based around scientific racism classified humans with the underlying assumption that racial differences reflected innate cultural and intellectual hierarchies. Clearly, such beliefs have a number of implications for both Māori women and men in terms of how we were perceived and constructed by Pākehā. Racist attitudes also served to heathenise Māori spirituality and to further eroticise Māori women. Māori women were frequently constructed as victims, entrapped within a primitive society and in dire need of 'transformation' and 'saving' by the missionary wives. To 'save' was a euphemism for ensuring women's chastity was maintained. The self-perceived 'respectable' woman sought to 'save' or 'de-eroticise' the 'unrespectable' woman – the Magdalene. Māori women were perceived as being naturally promiscuous and thus presented an enormous challenge to their 'saviours'.

Although the dichotomy of the two Marys springs from Catholicism, Māori women can nevertheless be viewed as being constructed as conforming to the Mary Magdalene prototype whether or not they had any direct contact with Catholic missionaries. As previously stated, the stereotypes of 'good' and 'bad' women were subjected to a variety of namings. The two Marys is only one such example. However, in places such as the Hokianga and the Whanganui River where Catholic missionaries impacted directly onto Māori communities, it is quite possible that the dichotomy of the two Marys had greater influence.

It would appear that these ideologies are strongly present in terms of how Māori women were perceived by Pākehā. During early periods of contact, explorers, whalers and sealers reinforced the Mary Magdalene construction by encouraging prostitution. However, attempts were made by missionaries to 'transform' Māori women into European models of ideal womanhood, and Māori women were subjected to Victorian ideologies of gender which promoted subservience and purity. Missionaries viewed Māori women as potential 'moral' and 'spiritual' reformers within Māori society, and 'agents of salvation' within the colonisation process with its policies of assimilation and Christianisation. Māori women were therefore constructed as both 'damned whores and God's police' concurrently. However, there was an unwritten proviso – we could only become God's police once we had become brown Pākehā and had learnt the ways of the 'one true God'. Our place in traditional Māori society which was determined more by rank than gender became, for many, as forgotten as the moa.

Historical constructions of Māori women, steeped in racism and cultural imperialism, eroded and fractured our sense of identity as Māori. The reconstruction of our identity served to alienate and displace us in much the same ways as assimilation and amalgamation policies have. However, although we can only hypothesise about the impact of this history on our contemporary sense of identity as Māori, it is feasible to speculate that the remnants of colonisation have been internalised at some level. Such a notion would in part explain why many Māori women (and indeed Māori men) have expressed ambivalence and confusion about articulating a sense of Māori identity.

Mana Wāhine Māori and Identity Politics

Mana wāhine Māori and identity politics has become a thorny issue within postcolonial Aotearoa/New Zealand as Māori women challenge assimilation policies and institutionalised racism that have marginalised and disempowered us. With reference to wāhine Māori, Kathie Irwin discusses how debates on identity have been destructive, divisive and immobilising:

> There is still destructive debate taking place is some quarters over who are 'real' and, heaven forbid, 'acceptable' Māori women. The discussions that go on about who is not a real Māori, or not Māori enough or only a weekend Māori, best serve the interests of those who wish to see us kept off the record and out of control.

Precious time is wasted debating amongst ourselves, who is and who isn't an 'acceptable' Māori. Trying to identify the 'ideologically correct, real Māori woman' has already proven futile ...[7]

Irwin's critique of the paralysis of identity politics provides a useful stimulus for reflecting on the struggles we face as Māori women working with other Māori women and also with tauiwi women. It highlights the potential for creating insider/outsider boundaries where there are those 'in the know' and those who are excluded from knowing. Such artificial boundaries create exclusions around our sense of identity which, as Irwin states, have already proven futile. It is not possible to define and locate a sense of personal identity as being universal to all Māori women. Differences in iwi and hapu, socialisation in a variety of whānau contexts, geographic location of residence, sexuality, political beliefs, level of formal education, knowledge of te reo Māori and tikanga Māori are all part of the experience of what it means to identify as wāhine Māori. However, although our individual experiences of what it means to identify as a Māori women may be quite diverse, it is possible to locate a collective identity. As Leonie Pihama states:

As individuals, we each have a place in terms of whakapapa and within whakapapa we are each connected to all those past and present.[8]

From this perspective, then, a degree of commonality could emerge which locates a collective identity, one which acknowledges the cosmological and earthly domains of Māoridom. To do this we must turn to our tūpuna and reflect on their ancient ways of knowing and their inherent wisdom. Ancient systems of knowledge knew no boundaries. The source of infinite wisdom was like an umbilical cord that connected us with nature and all the elements and was intertwined with whakapapa and ultimately our identity. Returning to the cosmological domains of our tūpuna raises a number of issues, yet it is the one connection we have to each other as Māori women.

Fragments of Stories

The three women ex-prisoners who participated in the research for my thesis were all healing themselves through a reconnection with their Māori heritage and culture, and as their identity as Māori evolved, so too did their acceptance of Māori spirituality, which ultimately strengthened them individually and collectively – a resurgence of the power of mana wāhine.

Several themes run through the fragments of experience which contributed to the constructions of identity for the three women. As children they all experienced some degree of 'otherness' – not knowing if they belonged in a Pākehā world or a Māori world. Ramare,[9] who grew up in the 1960s, had little knowledge of what it meant to be Māori. She didn't feel accepted by Māori, nor did she feel accepted by Pākehā: *'can remember growing up not belonging in a sense because I had Pākehā in me – you were always stuck in the middle and I grew up thinking I never belonged in either.'*

Kimiora, another woman in the study expressed similar sentiments: *'As a child I felt bad about being Māori – you were treated like you were dirty. I felt isolated. I stuck to myself as a child – felt I had no identity.'* This sense of isolation was part of Kimiora's life experience until her late twenties when she began to learn the Māori language: *'Learning te reo has given me an identity – I feel bad though because here's my own people giving me something back that should never have been taken away in the first place.'*

Māori identity has been profoundly influenced through a variety of historical and social discursive changes. Discourses of assimilation, for example, constructed a social and economic role for Māori that was subordinate to Pākehā. However, the discursive production of Māori identity changed radically during the 1970s with the Māori renaissance and Māori activism which challenged the philosophy and policies of assimilation. The stories of the women in the study demonstrated how their sense of identity was influenced both by these social movements and individual experiences.

Each woman's story was told to me through taped interview sessions and then in consultation with them the stories were rewritten in the third person. A brief extract Ramare's story centres on the evolution of her identity as Māori; it stems from her release from prison and a tramp through the Haurangi State Forest Park when she had a type of spiritual experience:

> *In a blinding flash of insight in the midst of Tane's great forest, amongst the trees; the Kauri, the Totara, the Rimu … amongst the birds; the tui, the kopara, piwakawaka … in the presence of Papatuanuku and Ranginui, she suddenly realised she was not lost:*
>
>> *I kore au e ngaro*
>> *ti kakano i ruia mai i Rangiatea*
>>
>> *I am never lost,*
>> *I am a seed sown at Rangiatea*
>
> *In that instant of insight she realised she could re-create her life. She could leave the underworld and she knew her tūpuna were showing her the way out. She could feel new life stirring deep within her. It was like a natural spring bursting forth from inside of her and overflowing with light, soft bubbles of joy … She offered a prayer to the atua residing in the bush; apologising that she did not know them by name and was unable to say a karakia in te reo Māori. The atua must have understood though as they have been with her ever since ….*

In Hiraina's story, her sense of Māori identity is traced through her love of a special taonga, a fish-hook pendant, given to her by her father:

> *As time went on her relationship with the matau kahurangi became more intimate. She no longer thought of him as an inanimate object. She would talk to him and in turn he would listen. He was never judgmental and little by little she began to tell him things she had never dared tell anyone else ….*

Telling the matau her childhood story revived all the old hurts and resentments but something began to change. Delicate new branches began to grow, tentatively reaching for the sky; seeking light and nourishment; drawing in sustenance. The young sapling began its transformation into a stout hearted Totara.

Totara manawa kaha,
tu pono ki te tika
Ruia, taitea kia tu ko taikaka

Stout hearted Totara,
standing straight and true
The sapwood surrounds the heart-wood beneath.

Her transformation was slow but the matau gave her courage to keep reaching towards the light. Slowly, she began to remove the mask she had shown to the world; slowly she began to reveal her real self.

And, 'who was her real self?', she would wonder each night as she lay alone in her cell in the narrow bed with its hard lumpy mattress, lying between the prison-issue sheets with their scorched linen smell, clutching the matau. She had despised herself for as long as she could remember, had thought of herself as nothing but a fat, useless, beat-up blob who deserved all she got. 'How did I let it happen?', 'how did I end up here?' she would whisper to the matau, again and again, and slowly the answers came to her.

In Kimiora's story, she traces her sense of having a Māori identity to learning the Māori language:

When she reclaimed her life, she reclaimed her Māori identity. Learning te reo was part of this reclamation. It had taken her a long time to find the confidence to apply for a course and she was totally committed to it. Over the last four months she had taken herself off to the little dining room each night to do her homework. She spent hours in there, studying and going over the day's lessons ... She thought about her classmates. They were all so different, yet the differences were all accepted. The bond of their Māori ancestry united them. She could feel the aroha when she walked into the classroom. Every morning began with a karakia and then they would kōrero with one another and she would feel the words flowing out of her in the language of her tūpuna. She would stand up and kōrero Māori and her body language would say all the rest:

Te kupu o te whatumanawa   *The heart-felt words, the body*
te kōrero o te tinana   *language reveal the path to your*
he whariki ki tona ngakau   *feelings*

The extracts from each of the women's stories focus on the reclamation of Māori identity and the resurgence of mana wāhine as a response to the effects of metaphorical and literal prisonisation. Reclaiming their cultural identity represented a step forward in a process of self healing.

The Impact of Mana Wāhine in the Context of Lives Reclaimed

Each of the three women in the research project had experienced both literal and metaphorical imprisonment. They had all been sentenced for crimes relating to either illegal substance abuse or prostitution. Growing up in the 1960s, they all spoke of being made to feel ashamed of being Māori; they all felt isolated and excluded as children. By the late 1970s however, discourses of Māori Renaissance were contesting the discourses of European supremacy and policies of assimilation and integration. In terms of race relations, there were multiple discourses offering competing and potentially contradictory ways of giving meaning to their lives. All three women chose to position themselves in relation to the discourses which resisted and challenged the hegemonic, hierarchical system of monoculturalism.

The construction of race cannot, however, be considered in isolation. Discourses on gender, constructions of femininity and sexuality, motherhood, class, education, penology, penal education, criminality of women and so on, impacted simultaneously on the ways the women made sense of their lives. The main focus of my research was to track the impact of mana wāhine in the context of lives reclaimed as each woman engaged in a process of self-healing. Their stories in full advocate the reclamation of one's cultural identity as one way of coming to terms with a variety of oppressions. However, although this process was viewed as a potentially empowering and necessary step towards self-healing, it was by no means seen as being a panacea for collective problems.

Nevertheless, the act of reclaiming our cultural heritage can not be undermined. Without exception, all the women developed a stronger sense of self in terms of personal identity and all expressed a deeper acceptance of the spiritual world and this in turn was reflected in an inner contentment and personal happiness that had previously been absent. Their stories also offer partial insights into experiences of dislocation of indigenous people who have been colonised, and they also give insights into experiences of oppression of victims of male violence.

The stories reflected how each participant's emotional responses to the world changed as they not only conceptualised it in different ways but also conceptualised themselves in different ways. Their ability to deal with anger, for example, was tied in with the complexities of rebuilding a sense of identity that validated and affirmed mana wāhine within a society which, although profoundly influenced by feminism and the language of biculturalism, is nevertheless fraught with ambiguities, tensions and contradiction. The intersections of race and gender are in a shifting dynamic and have been invoked with different meanings at particular historical moments. Consequently, our identities are being constantly realigned in response to these changes. Wendy Larner expands on this insight:

gender, colonial status, ethnicity, race and class are no longer seen as 'natural' identities. Rather, they are identities that are being constantly renegotiated and transformed in relation to shifting contexts made up of economic and social conditions, cultural and political institutions and ideologies.[10]

Discussion revolving around the construction of identity, although complex, is potentially empowering. The women in the study all became more aware of their own position in the world and realised they had the resources to resist the many dimensions of oppression. Their voices speak for all Māori women who have experienced prisonisation and they offer a particular response: the reclamation of mana wāhine. Such a response calls for an awareness of the connection between our life force and psyche, our spirituality and our personal power. Only then can a natural healing take place. The amelioration of the mauri and wairua will ultimately lead to a balanced state of harmony and equipoise, both individually and collectively. This is the state that each of the women in the study continue to strive for as they come to terms with their past and continue with their individual paths of healing and self determination. As the brief extracts from their stories demonstrate, such a state has in part been achieved through a reclamation of mana wāhine and reconnecting to Māori spirituality, and learning the language and the tikanga or culture.

Māori women have always had mana. The historical experiences of colonisation with its overlays of patriarchy, racism and capitalism resulted in a temporary suppression of mana for many women, but by no means for all. The resurgence of mana wāhine Māori evident in contemporary society is indicative of postcolonialism and the collective resistance of all indigenous people who are attempting to dismantle power structures that marginalised and eroded our cultural identity and mana. As we reclaim our cultural identities, we experience the power of mana wāhine ...

> Ko te hononga mauri
> Ko te hononga wairua
> Ko te hononga mana
> o te wāhine

Notes

1   D. Helene Connor, 'The Resurgence of Mana Wahine: A Response to "Prisonisation": Histories, Reflections and Stories' (MEd Thesis, University of Auckland, 1994).

2   At the time of writing, these were the most recent available figures from the Secretary of Justice and the Prison Census. According to the national census of 1996, Māori were 14.5 per cent of the New Zealand population.

3   Rosemary Ruether, 'Christianity', in Arvind Sharma (ed.), *Women in World Religion* (State University of New York Press, New York, 1987), p. 208.

4   Anne Summers, *Damned Whores and God's Police* (Penguin Books, 1975).

5   Cited in Raewyn Dalziel, 'The Colonial Helpmeet: Women's Role and the Vote in Nineteenth Century New Zealand', in B. Brookes, C. Macdonald and M. Tennant,

(eds), *Women in History, Essays on European Women in New Zealand* (Allen and Unwin, Wellington, 1986), p. 55.

6 Linda Tuhiwai Smith, 'Indigenous Women, the Problems of Positionality and the Pedagogies of Struggle', paper presented to the *Confronting Racism Conference – Conference on Racism, Indigenous Peoples, Ethnicity and Gender in Australia, New Zealand and Canada*, University of Technology, Sydney, 9-11 December, 1993, p. 4.

7 Kathie Irwin, 'Towards Theories of Maori Feminism', in Rosemary du Plessis (ed.), *Feminist Voices: Women's Studies Texts for Aotearoa/New Zealand* (Oxford University Press, Auckland, 1993), p. 3.

8 Leonie Pihama, 'No, I will not be a Post …', *Te Pua,* 2:1/2 (1993), p. 37.

9 These names are pseudonyms.

10 Wendy Larner, 'Changing Contexts: Globalisation, migration and feminism in New Zealand', in Sneja Gunew and Anna Yeatman (eds), *Feminism and the Politics of Difference* (Allen and Unwin, Sydney, 1993), p. 86.

TEN

Ancient Banyans, Flying Foxes and White Ginger:
The Poetry of Pacific Island Women

SELINA TUSITALA MARSH

Our writing is expressing a revolt against the hypocritical/exploitative aspects of our traditional/commercial/ and religious hierarchies, colonialism and neo-colonialism, and the degrading values being imposed from outside and by some elements in our societies.

Albert Wendt[1]

***

… I cannot
free myself from the clutches of poverty
firmly grasped in the skeletal touch
of my malnourished children

I cannot
escape the inescapable trappings
of my husband's dominance
and cultural bindings

I cannot
understand
why I cannot

Noumea Simi[2]

***

Samoan author Albert Wendt's seminal essay, 'Towards a New Oceania', opened up the flood gates for critical writing in the South Pacific in the early 1970s.[3] It celebrated the new era of decolonisation in a Pacific that had seen the uneventful arrival of Spanish explorers in the late sixteenth century, to the more life-changing imperial ships of Great Britain, United States, France, Germany, and Japan from the mid-nineteenth century onwards.[4] Island territories in the Pacific were explored and exploited for ideological escape and economic wealth. One of the many tools available to the coloniser – to subjugate, assimilate, and colonise indigenous minds – was education. However, Hawaiian poet, scholar, and sovereignty leader Haunani-Kay Trask called native agency within this imposed educational system the 'radicalised revolution' where, in varying degrees, colonial education backfired on its masters and was used to undermine, challenge and deconstruct imperialist master discourses. Literacy was one of the tools/weapons embraced by Pacific peoples. To paraphrase Salman Rushdie 'The Empire [began] ... writing back to the Centre'.[5] As the 'mini-empires' in the Pacific were being relinquished from the late 1960s onwards, indigenous peoples had much to say on colonialism pre- and post-independence.[6]

The internal 'elements' Wendt mentions in the quote above are taken up in Noumea Simi's poem 'I Cannot'. Simi, a Western Samoan poet and government official, tackles the internally oppressive elements of patriarchy and considers them next to wider international issues of colonialism. Simi poignantly illustrates the need for a framework of thinking to analyse wider issues of women's struggles, including all forms of dominance, social inequalities, and the role and influences of institutions. Ultimately, we need to know why 'we cannot' in order to question, challenge, and change situations that contribute to our oppression so that 'we can'. This article discusses how Pacific Island women poets acknowledge and address the tensions that arise from the 'double jeopardies' of race and gender in a 'post-colonial' era.[7] Their poetry reveals that multiple oppressions occur concurrently and in varying degrees at different times. Therefore, solutions and healing from these oppressions must be dealt with holistically, as opposed to subjecting women's experiences of oppression to linear models which invariably prioritise issues of race (colonialism) over gender (patriarchy) and gender over race.

A New Voyage

In 1973, Cook Islander, Marjorie Tuainekore Crocombe, member of the South Pacific Creative Arts Society, and founding editor of *Mana*,[8] proudly launched the Pacific's first international literary publication:

> The canoe is afloat. The flow of creativity in poetry, drama, storywriting, as well as other forms of creative expression from painting to wood sculpture has expanded enormously (in Oceania). Hidden talents are being developed, ideas are being expressed, confidence is growing, and the volume and quality increases all the time.[9]

This 'first wave' of Pacific literature took place in the late 1960s and 1970s culminating in the first Pacific anthology, *Lali: A Pacific Anthology of Pacific Literature written in English*, edited by Albert Wendt.[10] The lali, a type of drum found throughout the Pacific, is used as a form of communication and as a rhythmic instrument in celebration or mourning.[11] Wendt uses the lali as a metaphor for this burgeoning literature: 'A lali has a deep, booming sound. Commanding, definite; yet capable of many subtle nuances'.[12] This literature, like many indigenous literatures that emerged from colonialism, can be described as 'protest literature', often reactionary and written against a history of colonial domination and exploitation that had silenced indigenous voices. The islands fresh from gaining their independence were scathing of colonialism, mournful of cultural losses, and heavily committed to resurrecting their proud indigeneity. 'Consequently,' Wendt observes, 'much of it is a fabulous storehouse of anthropology, sociology, art, religion, history, dance and music'.[13] Others, on the verge of achieving independence in the late 1970s, were anxious, and nervous with restrained energy. Sporadically, intense political conflicts overflowed into violence.[14] In early Pacific literature, the writing tended to be angry, nationalistic, and heavily pessimistic in tone. Colonial and indigenous people were seen in 'irreconcilable opposition'.[15]

A lull in the writing occurred in the mid-seventies. The 'educated' literate group behind the initial burst of creativity were now prime candidates for leadership positions in their newly Independent nations. Appointments in government, education and business were created and filled. Writing was quickly eclipsed by more urgent national priorities, in many cases never to surface again.

Ironically, some of the writers became the embodiment of the colonial 'evil' they had protested about. Although colonial administrators gave way to 'native sons', in many islands the oppressive power structures remained intact. Within this system, these new 'civil servants' were easily corrupted by power, money and eurocentricity:

> Many of my friends
> Are civil servants
> With uncivil thoughts …
> … But they cannot erase my existence
> For my plight chimes with the hour
> And my blood they drink at cocktail parties
> Always full of smiling false faces
> Behind which lies authority and private interests … [16]

The 'false gleam' of independence noted in other 'post'-colonial societies was just as evident in the Pacific.[17] Independence was not a magic formula to end all suffering. This post-independence disillusionment was reflected in much Pacific literature.

A second wave of writing began again in the 1980s, and was manifested in a second anthology, *Nuanua: Pacific Writing in English Since 1980*, in 1995, also edited by Wendt. Nuanua, meaning rainbow in many Pacific languages, retains its biblical symbolism of hope and promise inherent in a new era of decolonisation in the Pacific. By now, all the islands represented in the anthology had achieved either self-governance or full independence.[18] The apt rainbow image celebrates distinction and unity of colour while metaphorically celebrating distinct voices and cultures in the Pacific after the rain/reign of colonialism.

Writing focused largely on themes of colonialism and neo-colonialism, racism, tradition versus modernity, internal political corruption, cultural clashes, still with a strong sense of profound loss.[19]

Although significantly fewer in number, women's voices were present in both representative anthologies. In *Lali*, seven out of forty-four writers were women. Fifteen years later, *Nuanua* published sixty-five writers, eighteen of whom were women. Pacific women have written and been published alongside Pacific men since 1948, but relatively little is known of their work beyond the Pacific Islands.[20] Certainly New Zealand and Australian literary circles seem largely oblivious to the neighbouring voices chanting from a region occupying one third of the world's surface where one quarter of the world's languages are spoken.[21]

Four Poets

The four poets discussed here are the first women in their islands to be published in English and are relatively well known throughout the South Pacific Islands. These women were the first to submit a specifically female Pacific Island voice. The preface of Solomon Island poet Jully Makini's first collection of poetry, *Civilised Girl*, explicitly notes this inaugural voicing, this breaking of silence in the light of an historical absence of a woman's point of view:

> This collection is a first in several ways: it's Jully's first published work and some of the first writing of Solomon Islands women; and it's the first time that one is able not only to hear or sense a woman's views on certain matters but also to see them in print in a complete book in this country.

The collection was published in 1981, three years after the Solomons' gained independence from the British. *Civilized Girl* critiqued a spectrum of inequalities, from the corrupted privilege of civil servants to 'the inequalities of Solomon Islands life for women'.[22] A year later, Makini worked with the University of South Pacific Solomon Islands Extension Centre and co-edited the Solomons' first anthology of writing by women. *Mi Mere: Poetry and Prose by Solomon Islands Women Writers* was published in 1983.[23] Makini's informative and explicit afterword aptly summarises the publication:

> Mi Mere   – I am a women struggling to tell the world about my plight; educated, privileged, a lucky one – seen and not heard.
>
> Mi Mere   – I am a women who never went to school, destined to stay in the village for the rest of my life – seen and not heard.
>
> Mi Mere   – A book of stories, poems and photographs about Solomon Islands women and their concerns.
>
> Mi Mere   – A book by Solomon Islands women for men and women who want to understand.[24]

The diversity of whose stories are being told, to whom, and the difficult journeys made to get from private experience to public voice are made apparent in this collection. Voices range from urban to rural women, from highly educated in the Western world, to having little exposure to Western influences, all convey the need to voice their concerns, issues, and plights. The courage in doing so can not be under-estimated.[25]

The women writers discussed in this essay are well educated and well travelled. Tongan poet, Konai Helu Thaman, was educated in Tonga, New Zealand, Fiji and the United States. She has a B.A. in Geography, a teaching degree, an M.A. in International Education, and a Ph.D in Education. She is currently Professor of Pacific Education and Culture at the University of the South Pacific in Suva, Fiji. Thaman is one of the most prolific and established Pacific poets and has five publications to date.[26] Samoan artist and poet, Momoe Malietoa Von Reiche, was educated in New Zealand and taught art at a Teacher's Training College and Polytech in New Zealand.[27] She is currently curator and artist-in-residence at Madd Gallery (Apia, Western Samoa), Samoa's only established alternative art space. Von Reiche has produced three collections of poetry.[28] Grace Mera Molisa, ardent Ni-Vanuatu politician, poet and activist, was schooled in New Zealand and holds a university degree. She was pivotal in organising the First South Pacific Women's Conference in Suva, Fiji (1975), became the first woman to hold a senior government position and was heavily involved in the move for Independence. She is a prolific writer and has organised several art conferences. Molisa formed her own publication house, Black Stone, and has three publications to date.[29] Jully Makini, from the Kindu tribe in Gizo, Solomon Islands, has also recieved an international education and was awarded an East-West Centre scholarship which allowed her to produce her second collection of poetry *Praying Parents.*

While these women emerged from their island communities (and some remain within them) they are in no way meant to be representative of all Pacific women. They are comparatively 'élite'. But each has used her education and writing to voice many concerns women in their islands have long held. Each poet, in her unique way, has endeavoured to publicise the private and politicise the personal.

Poets Speak

The Kingdom of Tonga is unique in that it continued to be governed by its own constitutional monarchy throughout colonialism in the South Pacific.[30] Although it was never 'formally' colonised, poet, academic and teacher Konai Helu Thaman, acknowledges the colonial mentality still absorbed from foreign influences in her cascading poem 'I Tremble':

I tremble
At the thought
Of going to town
And meeting brutal men
Who think that white is clean
And black is dirty ... [31]

Its accelerating intensity moves from potential sexism to realised racist sexism as the narrator finds herself subject to white (or whitened) male gazes. Violence lurks beneath her lines as the narrator trembles in fear and trepidation of travelling beyond the safety of 'home'. As the poem progresses, we realise that the trembling is not just a result of fear, but is a more universal shudder for the degradation of a power-hungry and increasingly insecure humanity.

Generally, Thaman's early work focuses upon inter-cultural tensions created by modernisation, the threat of change, and abuses of customary power. Thaman uses a subtle, understated style to pare away public hypocrisy and expose the 'truth', as evident in her short poem 'My Neighbour':

My neighbour is
A very generous man
He pays school fees
Of needy children
Every year
Provides feasts
For his church
And is a supporter
Of women's rights –
Yet I can never understand
Why he frequently
Beats up his wife. [32]

Similar issues are subtly alluded to in Samoa's poet and artist Momoe Malietoa Von Reiche's highly personalised poetry. Samoa, formerly 'German Samoa' prior to World War I,[33] gained its Independence from a New Zealand protectorate in 1969.[34] Of that time, Von Reiche recalls in her poem 'Solaua, a secret embryo':

... German tyranny
And Chinese indentured labour ...
And ancient banyans,
Flying foxes and white ginger.[35]

Von Reiche, describing one of the places where she lived in Apia, also realises her colonial German connections.[36] Solaua, the 'place of rains', is a valley replete with cattle and horses ('She can smell / Cowdung in the mist of

/ Solaua') farmed on an old colonial German-owned ranch. Physically encapsulated, like a protective embryo surrounded by life-giving waters, Solaua also contains embryo-secrets awaiting birth. The land is more than a colonial piece of real-estate. It holds the sweat of exploited migrant labour which used to work the land. It also possesses an age-old pre-colonial connection to the land of 'ancient banyans', symbolising timeless genealogy as its sprouting branches continually root into earth to become tree trunks that, in turn, sprout new branches.

For the poem's female persona, Solaua is 'where her heart / is suspended / From a rubber tree'. This complex image is a metaphor for mixed marriages, or loyalties crossing over difference.[37] Here, the difference is race. The narrator betrays a certain complicity with German colonialists symbolised by the presence of the non-native rubber tree that has firmly taken root in the land – and in her heart. In a romantic and a historically race-tensioned sphere, she has been betrayed by her heart. However, amidst these complex tensions, her homeland is able to give her some sense of security and closure. At Solaua, her erotic relationship with the fanua (the land, also means 'placenta' and thus another reference to birth) is consummated: 'She lusts for the earth so / Completely there'.

Von Reiche continues the theme of land, still physically and emotionally reminiscent of colonial occupation, in her poem 'Above the Gully of Your Childhood':

> The old homestead still looked
> Gracious in the half light,
> Although the slats reeked
> Of a once foreign woman
> Who served teas
> On the patio in her colonial willow patterns.
> Her once distinguished
> Planter husband excelled
> In elaborate ceremony –
> But had a weakness
> For brown bosoms. [38]

This snapshot of the colonial era is distinctly taken from a woman's point of view. A gendered 'connection' between women is made across differences of race and class (and rank). The narrator of the poem can empathise to a certain extent with the colonist who, although 'foreign', is also woman – in this instance, a woman overshadowed by her public, ceremonial-centred, adulterous planter husband. Von Reiche makes her visible in her social invisibility. The bond in the poem between these two women is formed from a common and universal experience that supersedes racial and social categories: the betrayal of adultery. The narrator in the poem finds a joint source of commiseration across difference. This theme of cross-cultural infidelity is found throughout Von Reiche's work.[39]

Crossing cultures and poetical emphasis, we move from the highly personal to the overtly political poetry of poet, politician and grassroots activist Grace Mera Molisa. Vanuatu, formerly the 'New Hebrides' or 'Nouvelle Hebrides' depending upon one's British or French persuasion, gained its Independence from this unique Joint Condominium in 1980.[40] Molisa is comically scathing in her critique of this colonial Joint 'Pandemonium'.[41] The remnants of expatriate political 'pests' left behind in her tongue-in-cheek, word-play poem give new meaning to 'Interference':

Fleeing

fleas

extra patria

politicking

poly ticks

fleecing

lice

lousing

sticky

beaks

poking

politicks.[42]

In typical ascending/descending pinnacle form, Molisa layers meaning beneath the semblance of worded simplicity. In 'Statelessness', Molisa pares down imagery to its essential bareness in meaning and space, re-iterating the stateless person, alone, without rightful inheritance after the legalities of colonialism:

> I
>
> the
>
> native
>
> aboriginal
>
> autochthone
>
> heir begotten
>
> of mother earth
>
> legislated stateless.[43]

Elsewhere, Molisa's poetry uses deeply embedded cultural metaphors (black stone) as a reclamation of pre-contact existence that is still secure.

In similar pinnacle layout that echoes the volcanic foundations of many islands, Solomon Island poet, grassroots activist and journalist Jully Makini (formerly Sipolo)[44] observes the aftermath of British colonialism that officially came to an end in 1978. Makini pays particular attention to the eurocentric ideological dominance over Native female identity. In her almost voyeuristic poem 'Civilized Girl', Makini proceeds to 'dismember', and thus deconstruct, colonial and patriarchal constructions of desirable femininity:

> Cheap perfume
> Six inch heels
> Skin-tight pants
> Civilized girl.

This disembodied picture of the 'post-colonial woman' reveals the shallowness of an identity based upon the accumulation of Western accoutrements and Western-defined dictates of womanhood and beauty. Makini critiques an uncritical adoption/adaptation of Western standards of beauty and intricately relates it to the process of colonialism. The unnatural plucking and primping leads to an identity crisis, and an uncertainty of the future:

Who am I?
Melanesian Caucasian or
Half-caste?
Make up your mind
Where am I going –
Forward, backward, still?
What do I call myself –
Mrs, Miss or Ms? [45]

This 'Civilized Girl', is dressed in all the Western signs of beauty: perfume, high heels, newly softened hair, plucked and primped, painted and poked, in the last stanza proclaims:

Why do I do this?
Imitation
What's wrong with it?
Civilization.

The two key words emphasised in the last stanza by alliteration are 'Imitation' and 'Civilization'. Civilization can be read as a justification for the 'dressing up' and 'acting up' of the woman. More likely, the seeking of civilisation by imitating Western notions of femininity has led to her identity crisis. In bell hooks' terms, this 'civilized' girl has 'internalized with supremacist values and aesthetics, a way of looking and seeing the world that negates her value'.[46] Makini critiques the false new imaging sought out by some Pacific women (and endorsed by some Pacific men!) who fall into the eurocentric trap of believing that beforehand they were not 'civilized', and arguably questions whether the notion and goal of an imposed definition of 'civilization' is desirable in the first place.

Although the popularly used geographical distinction is problematic,[47] there does seem to be a difference in poetic intensity, the degree of didacticism in dealing with subject matter, and c/overt allusion to subtext between the Polynesian and Melanesian poets. Arguably, these variances reflect not only different cultural aesthetics, but distinct political contexts. Generally, Independence in Melanesia was accorded later and, as was the case in Vanuatu, often violently.[48] The political polemic typical of 'first wave' oppositional writing against colonialism thus tends to be slightly more concentrated and obvious in this Melanesian writing.

In both regions, however, much creative writing by Pacific Islands women joins in unison with that of Pacific men in critiquing, deconstructing, and mourning colonialism, the celebration of nationhood, the complexities of independence, the influence of modernity and the loss of tradition. But as is equally apparent in the poems previously discussed, there are important departures dictated by a female point of view. I want now to turn to a particularly distinct and important area in Pacific women's writing, the often conflicting intersection of the external oppression of colonialism and the internal oppression of patriarchy.

Intersecting '-isms': Racism and Sexism

It is ironic that the official unsilencing – 'decolonisation' – fostered other silences in the creation of 'new' nations. Over time it became clear, particularly after Independence celebrations, that nationalism wore a patriarchal mask. Because most politicians were male, exploitation of the people, and abuses of power, were most actioned by men, and most suffered by women.[49]

As Thaman points out in her poem 'My Blood', it is the 'brother' who is now the oppressive neo-colonial 'Other':

> You tell me that I've been 'exploited'
> And that I must rebel NOW;
> You tell me that I must be their equal
> You tell me that if I don't
> I am sick, apathetic and useless …
>
> No brother …
> My problem is not 'exploitation'
> Or unequal pay, or unawareness;
> My problem is that I
> Have been betrayed and trampled on
> By my own blood.
> Don't forget YOU are their product
> And YOU must sell. [50]

Patriarchal nationalism is a global phenomenon. Women were often silenced for the greater cause of the nation.[51] Justifiably in many instances, it was argued that a fractured focus in newly unified nationalist movements had the potential to weaken a movement based upon unity of race in the face of a larger racist foe. Internal divisions were perceived as internal weaknesses. Thus, in the (continuing) era of decolonisation and movements of independence, gender concerns are/were often second to those of race.

An often-used argument for de-prioritising the 'women question' in post-colonial societies is the 'first things first' position. This argument posits that national liberation must take precedence over infrastructural matters, including women's liberation. It is a strategy which is mono-focal and based upon a linear model of responding to oppression. And it 'forgets' that women often comprise over half of the nation as it separates, de-prioritises and binarises national liberation over women's liberation.

It is instructive to take a momentary detour and journey from the Pacific to the African continent and eavesdrop on a pertinent conversation. Malawian poet Felix Mnthali takes part in an ongoing discussion considering which issue should take priority: the fight for female equality or the fight against Western cultural imperialism? His poem 'Letter to a Feminist Friend', was written to fellow countrywoman and academic, Molara Ogundipe-Leslie, English Literature Professor. It follows in its entirety:

> My world has been raped
> looted
>   and squeezed
>
>   by Europe and America ...
>
> AND NOW
>
> the women of Europe and America
> after drinking and carousing
> on my sweat
> rise up to castigate
> and castrate
> their menfolk
> from the cushions of a world
> I have built!
>
> Why should they be allowed
> to come between us?
> You and I were slaves together
> uprooted and humiliated together
> Rapes and lynchings ...
>
> do your friends 'in the movement'
> understand these things? ...
>
> No, no, my sister,
> my love,
> Too many gangsters
> still stalk this continent ...
>
> When Africa
> at home and across the sea
> is truly free
> there will be time for me

and time for you
to share the cooking
and change the nappies –
till then,
first things first!

In reply, Ogundipe-Leslie points out the masculine first person possessive used to speak for the nation: 'The Promethean person who endured slavery and the slave trade, colonialism, imperialism, and neocolonialism does not have time for women's rights yet. The world has been built by *him* and *he* must attend to those pressing issues'.[52] Indeed, it is *his* world that has been 'raped / looted / and squeezed'. It is a world which *he* has built. The universalised male 'I' persona, is further highlighted when considering that the poem directly addresses itself to an indigenous (fellow-native) female subject. Although 'she' is recognised as having suffered at the hands of colonial oppression, she is not acknowledged as having taken part in nationalist struggles, nor in indigenous formations of the world.

Feminism and the struggle for the liberation of women has been stigmatised as 'foreign', 'inconsequential', and 'frivolous' by its singularly Westernised reduction to sharing the housework and changing nappies. Mnthali equates feminism with the *feminisation* of men and thus their degradation. In doing so, he reproduces a colonial trope where colonised men are often feminised. One effect of this is that voice and representation of colonised women within the anti-colonial discourse is, once again, appropriated.[53]

Ogundipe-Leslie firmly debunks this linear model of dealing with oppression using international examples:

> Somehow, miraculously, you can liberate a country and later turn your attention to the women of that country – first things first! But such liberators of nations as Lenin, Mao, Machel, Neto, and Cabral, among others, knew that no basic and effective change can occur in a society without the *synchronic liberation of its women*. [italics added][54]

From America to Afghanistan to Algeria, women from all over the world have demanded such synchronisation but continually find themselves sandwiched between rival forces that exploit either their voices, or their silences.[55] The 'women question' (women's work and improvement of her status) has all too often been shunted aside to make room for more urgent 'national' matters at hand i.e. 'to liberate the land, *then* the women'.[56] Although it is understandable that certain focuses must take precedence, it is all too easy to sweep this issue aside and cast it on to a perpetual 'to deal with' pile.[57] The 'women question' remains an ever-elusive, easily postponed agenda in government.

Meanwhile, women have fought alongside men in struggling for independence but are neither acknowledged nor rewarded with the same quality of benefits.[58] Some argue the only way that women's liberation will gain the acknowledgment it deserves is to organise 'outside of male-conceived and male-controlled master plans of development'.[59] This involves women claiming the freedom to define their own terms and create paths of development that meet their needs and desires.

While many Pacific women recognise that there is little chance for effective change without men, there is a need for 'male-conceived' and 'male-controlled' ideological structures to be 'feminised' – that is, for women's active input in policies at all levels of society. Indeed, Pacific women are increasingly making it clear that women need to be involved in more of the decision-making processes in their islands, especially when the quality of their own lives is directly influenced.[60]

There is a recurring pattern throughout the globe concerning women and the part they play in nationalist movements for independence. Policies are often introduced which 'unsilence' women, to enable them to fight for nationalist causes. However, once the fight has been won, women are again silenced. Unsilencing in the face of nationalism entails: recognising oppression and being aware of ongoing imperial and/or patriarchal 'colonisation'; debunking linear 'first thing's first' types of argument; holding the government accountable for promises of post-independent liberation; recognising and acknowledging previous catalysts for change, i.e. the woman warriors who have gone before and have yet to be acknowledged; defining policies formed by the needs, desires and concerns of *both* men and women. Achieving such aims will involve altering masculine paradigms.

Words Change

The poetry of these Pacific women goes some way towards realising such steps by raising public consciousness about the internal oppressions suffered by 'mothers of the nation' in, through and after colonisation. Issues of colonialism and patriarchy are experienced at certain times in different degrees. To illustrate the varying 'degrees' of colonialism and patriarchy as experienced by women, I want to return to the vociferous poetry of Ni-Vanuatu poet Grace Mera Molisa. Of particular note is Molisa's poetic development and the degree of thematic emphasis she places between collections in order to reflect this colonial/ patriarchal complexity experienced by women throughout the Pacific.

Molisa's first two collections differ in thematic emphasis. Post-colonialism, Independence and nationhood are the primary themes of Molisa's first publication_*Black Stone* (1983). Its dedication is made to:

> our nameless
> numberless
> ancestors

who waged
isolated
battles
for integrity
and freedom
enabling
our generation
to harvest
the fruit
of their
labour.

Finally, the people of Vanuatu are 'free' from colonial shackles. 'Vanuatu', the first poem in the collection, glories in new-found nationhood, recalling the 'bitter – sweet / fruit / of sovereignty struggle'. 'Black Stone', the hardened volcanic lava of Vanuatu's numerous active volcanoes and the source of its vatu (land), is Molisa's primary metaphor for the new nation state of Ni-Vanuatu. It is used as the title for two of her three collections. The black volcanic foundation also reflects the timelessness and solidity of Ni-Vanuatu. Molisa recalls:

Ageless Vatu
primeval source
of creative forces
ad infinitum ...

... Vatu offspring
born of oblivion
in vexing rebellion
stay steadfast
Vanuaaku Vanuatu.

Similar metaphors are used in her poem 'Black Stone' to describe Ni-Vanuatu. The vatu and its people are 'solidified', 'coagulated', 'hard', 'obstinate', and 'indelible'. Having survived two colonial powers, vatu and Ni-Vanuatu are summarised as 'immovable, immobile'. They have survived, they have remained. The Vanuaaku Pati, the indigenous political party with which Molisa was heavily involved before and after independence, was promoted to the people as being comprised of the 'true' people of the land (as opposed to transient colonists and foreigners). It is defended as stemming from the 'rural mass movement' as opposed to the 'self-interested petty bourgeois dissident urban fringe' in Molisa's poem 'Victim of Foreign Abuse'.

Molisa's metaphor of inured, ageless volcanic rock reflects the political and cultural stability of Vanuatu. In comparison, volcanic lava is fluid, transitional, and dangerous in the work of Hawaiian poet, scholar, sovereignty leader, Haunani-Kay Trask. On one level, this reflects the on-going colonial situation of Hawai'i which remains a colony of the United States. Yet to achieve sovereignty and the addressing of past wrongs,[61] Hawaiians are unable to boast the political and cultural solidarity of Independent Vanuatu in relation to its colonial past. The political situation remains unstable and smouldering beneath indigenous resentment and protest:

> Cracked lava stones
> flesh with tears, sprout
> thorny vines, thick
> and foreign[62]

Here, lava is prevented from hardening, its wounds continually open afresh. Fresh, molten lava, rather than birthing new land, sheds bitter tears caused by foreign colonial invasion symbolised by imported plants which often over-grow and choke their indigenous hosts.[63]

While Independence is focused upon in *Black Stone*, this collection also contains Molisa's most renowned and celebrated poem 'Custom'. It is one among several poems that criticise selective patriarchal pickings and constructions of culture, much to the detriment of women.[64] Molisa critiques those who are:

> Inadvertently
> misappropriating
> 'Custom'
> misapplied
> bastardised
> murdered
> a frankenstein
> corpse
> conveniently
> recalled
> to intimidate
> women
> the timid
> the ignorant
> the weak.

'Custom' addresses and challenges both imperialism and patriarchy. With the advent of colonialism, customs were ignored, rejected, transformed, retained, or belittled. Through her poetry Molisa contends that many remaining customs served to reinforce oppressive male power structures and sanction violence against women. Molisa is not rejecting custom *per se*, but problematises notions like 'tradition' and challenges the reader to critically see ideas usually taken for granted under the banner of 'culture'. Such 'notions' are often subject to historical and political construction and manipulation. Elsewhere, Molisa acknowledges the value of traditional indigenous ways of knowing and being that are sincerely honoured.[65]

In 1987 Molisa published her second collection, *Colonised People*. Its ironic title and dedication indicates a significant shift in focus:

> 'TO THE WOMEN OF VANUATU
> who toil and labour daily, unrecognised, unrewarded,
> just to cope with life's chores and burdens
> and to THE HOPE that Future Generations of Vanuatu
> Women
> will be able to enjoy a better Life.'

In a dramatic shift, the colonised people are no longer the people of Vanuatu, but its women. Molisa makes this explicit in the introduction: 'Vanuatu is now free of foreign colonial domination but Ni-Vanuatu Women are still colonised'. The poem entitled 'Vanuatu' in this collection demonstrates Molisa's political awareness and her familiarity with, and contempt for, empty rhetoric.

In contrast to 'Vanuatu' in *Black Stone* which celebrates post-colonial Independence, 'Vanuatu' in this collection challenges the lofty principles of 'Democracy', 'Christianity', and 'Melanesian Values' established in the Independence 'fervour'. Also noticeably altered is Molisa's trademark vertical pinnacle layout used throughout her poetry.[66] Thus, the layout of this poem is significant and follows in its entirety:

VANUATU

Vanuatu is:

FREE	Men are Free,
	Women are chattels
SELF-DETERMINED	Men determine,
	Women go along
INDEPENDENT	Women Depend on Men
ENJOYING THE FRUITS	
OF THE STRUGGLE	For Men Only

The Nature of the Nation's Democracy

The Nature of the Nation's Christianity

The Nature of the Nation's Melanesian Values

Is Exemplified in Practice

Its antithetical layout emphasises the opposition between national rhetoric of freedom, independence and self government on the left hand side, and the reality of the continuing oppressive situation of women in relation to men at the right hand side of the poem. Perhaps the reading of each side can be summarised as 'rhetoric' versus 'reality'. The words on the left hand side are capitalised to mark their 'authority'. The predominant use of lower case letters on the right, arguably symbolise the 'unofficial' version of truth. Thus, while Vanuatu is 'SELF-DETERMINED / Men determine / Women go along'.[67]

The visual layout is ironic. Ideally, balance of form symbolises equality, parity and harmony. The implicit message conveyed visually and literally is that women, while officially included in the equalising rhetoric of post-colonial freedom, still remain subject to the abusive power of men. As the symbolic placement of the first two couplets on the right side suggest, women continue to be placed *second* to men; women continue to be placed *beneath* men.

Additionally, the symmetrical layout structurally emphasises the nature of the culture/gender dilemma. The poem emphasises the opposition between the national rhetoric of freedom, independence and self government, and the reality of women who *at the same time* remain exploited and oppressed by their men. For indigenous women, freedom and independence simultaneously occur with oppression. The structural form of the poem is deliberately composed to indicate that women remain oppressed *in* and *through* this rhetoric. Molisa takes the root word from the left-hand side and uses it to 'germinate' sentences on the right. She metaphorically indicates that while there is some truth to what is being publicly said, it is not fully being realised by women. The different context of the word used on the right gives its meaning an ironic twist. The similar image of the 'bitter – sweet / fruit / of sovereignty struggle' in her poem 'Vanuatu' (first collection) is linked and compared with reaping the 'FRUITS / OF THE STRUGGLE' in 'Vanuatu' (second collection). Unfortunately, Molisa indicates that the fruit of Independence has turned sour because it has proved to be 'For Men Only'. It rots with the realisation that women remain 'Colonised People'.

Ideally, the future lies in the middle with a balance of left and right, capital and lower case, the government and the people, man and woman. Molisa argues that such a com/promise will build up and restore Vanuatu.

Molisa's poem 'Vanuatu' also appeared in a publication she organised in 1991 titled *Woman Ikat Raet O No?* ('Have Women Got Rights or Not?') informing ni-Vanuatu women of the ratification of the United Nations declaration. On the inside cover, a quote from the United Nations states that: 'the full and complete development of a country, the welfare of the world and the cause of peace require the maximum participation of women on equal terms with men in all fields'.[68] Molisa challenges the 'complete development' of Vanuatu as hailed in its Independence celebrations. 'Vanuatu' dominates a full page and appears in forceful oppositional colours, consisting of white letters on a framed black background. As in Molisa's previous work, black is a significant colour. Its use asserts that this additional battle is being fought on 'black stone', on the vatu (land) of a people who should be united in this struggle.[69] At the bottom of the page, the poem is signed and overtly owned by Molisa. Both publications testify that independence has failed to address the oppressive situation of women.

Through a clever play of words, form and structure, and a relentless commitment to fulfilling her self-proclaimed role of the artist as community conscience and mouthpiece, Molisa articulated then (1987) and now (1990s) the situation of Vanuatu from the point of view of many women.[70]

In Molisa's poetry, the problem with the 'first things first' argument is that 'second' things are rarely given first priority. More often than not, women's concerns continue to get swept aside after national independence has been realised. The achievement of independence is not a 'once and for all' event, but more like a continuous revelation. The concerns of the nation and the concerns of women are not mutually exclusive. Recognition of these 'internal others' suffering from 'internal oppressions' need not fracture the focus of resistance to universal sources of oppression like colonialism or neo-colonialism. The solution lies in a holistic approach that views oppression as multi-faceted, and as such, demands multi-faceted approaches defined and executed by the commitment of men *and* women. The need to recognise and deal with the double exploitation is seen by Kanaky (New Caledonia) Susanna Ounei-Small as absolutely essential in the fight for Independence: 'The priority for Kanaky women must be to struggle together with Kanak men, while trying to change their violent and sexist behaviour.'[71]

The poetry of the Pacific Island women discussed in this article acknowledges the synchronisation of external and internal oppressions suffered by women in the Pacific. Colonialism and patriarchy occur concurrently and thus need to be dealt with holistically. Now that independence has been achieved in many islands we must, with increasing commitment, turn our focus to the voices that cry oppression if we are not to perpetuate that oppression, if inequitable structures created (or exacerbated) through colonialism are not to be repeated and internalised. This is the challenge in the work of these Pacific Island women poets.

Notes

1   Albert Wendt, 'Towards A New Oceania', *Mana Review: A South Pacific Journal of Language and Literature*, 1:1 (1976), pp. 49-60.

2   Noumea Simi, *Waves of Dawn: La Folau o le Vaveao* (Samoa Observer NZ Ltd, Apia, Western Samoa, 1992), p. 35.

3   Albert Wendt was/is also an important figure in inspiring and leading the creative writing scene in the Pacific with his ground breaking novels: *Sons For The Return Home* (Longman Paul, Auckland, 1973); *Leaves of the Banyan Tree* (Longman Paul, Auckland, 1979); and *Pouliuli* (Penguin Books, Auckland, 1987). Wendt has since published numerous novels, short stories and poetry, and edited several anthologies and collections of Pacific writing.

4   Previously unsuccessful colonial expeditions in the Pacific were made by the Spanish in the beginning of the Sixteenth Century. See I.C. Campbell, *A History of the Pacific Islands* (Canterbury University Press, Christchurch, 1989), p. 128.

5   Bill Ashcroft, Gareth Griffiths, and Helen Tiffen, *The Empire Writes Back: Theory and Practice in Post-Colonial Literatures* (Routledge, London, New York, 1989), p. viii.

6   Despite some Island nations achieving independence from 1960s onwards, in 1997 many have yet to realise indigenous sovereignty. Even today, the hailed arrival of our 'post-colonial' era sounds hollow. Many argue that 'colonialism' is alive and well today via covert ownership and control of Island nations by multinational corporations, and organisations like the World Bank and the International Monetary Fund. Many Pacific peoples remain actively involved in fighting for their sovereignty against the colonial giants of America (Hawai'i), France (many parts of Micronesia), and Australia (Aboriginal tribes). Also, the 'I' of independence is capitalised when referring to a specific political movement.

7   This term was coined by early African-American feminist socialist Angela Davis in *Women, Race and Class* (Random House, New York, 1981). This becomes 'multiple jeopardies' with consideration of class, creed, sexual orientation, etc.

8   A pivotal journal of creative writing instrumental in fostering and disseminating writing in and around the South Pacific.

9   *Mana Annual* (Fiji, Pacific Creative Arts Society, 1973 & 1974) as quoted in Signey M. Mead and Bernie Kernot (eds), *Art and Artists of Oceania* (Dunmore Press, Palmerston North, 1983).

10 Albert Wendt (ed.), *Lali: A Pacific Anthology* (Longman Paul, Auckland, 1980), back cover.

11 The lali is formed from a piece of hollowed-out tree trunk, and beaten with heavy wooden sticks.

12 Wendt, *Lali: A Pacific Anthology*, p. 3.

13 Albert Wendt (ed.), *Nua Nua: Pacific Writing in English Since 1980* (Auckland University Press, Auckland, 1995), p. 4.

14 For example, the situation of Vanuatu, and the Solomon Islands. See I.C. Campbell, *A History of the Pacific Islands* (Canterbury University Press, Christchurch, 1989).

15 Ibid.

16 Konai Helu Thaman, 'Uncivil Servants', *You, The Choice Of My Parents* (Mana Publications, Suva, 1974), p. 8.

17 Nigerian writer Ngugi' wa Thiongo called post-Independence disenchantment and disillustionment in the context of Nigerian independence the 'false gleam'. See his award-winning novel *Petals of Blood* (Heinemann, London, 1977).

18 The islands represented in the anthology *Nuanua* are Cook Islands, Fiji, Kiribati, Niue, Papua New Guinea, Samoa, Solomon Islands, Tonga, Vanuatu. Not included and still to achieve Independence (or some form of self-government) are the Hawaiians and Aborigines.

19 Wendt, p. 6.

20 The first known publication by a Pacific Islands woman was Cook Islander Florence 'Johnny' Frisbie's *Miss Ulysses From Puka-Puka: The Autobiography of a South Seas Trader's Daughter* (Macmillan, New York, 1948), the autobiographical story of a young girl growing up in Puka Puka. Unfortunately, the promise of more writing from women in the Pacific in any substantial form would not be fulfilled until the second wave of Pacific writing in the 1980s. The book was written and published with the aid of Frisbie's white trader father.

21 Campbell, p. 11.

22 Takiora Ingram Pryor, 'Solomon's Bold Poet Jully Makini', *Pacific Magazine*, 12:5 (1987), Issue 65, September/October, p. 55.

23 Jully Sipolo (ed.), *Mi Mere: Poetry and Prose* (University of the South Pacific, Solomon Islands Centre, Honiara, Solomon Islands, 1983).

24 'Mi Mere' can be translated as 'Me Woman'. Note, this is in the singular, thus avoiding any indication that this is a homogenous group.

25 A note at the beginning of the collection explains the choice of some writers who 'choose to remain anonymous because of the very real constraints on freedom of expression by women which still exist in Solomon Islands societies' (Sipolo, p. vi).

26 Thaman, *You, The Choice of My Parents* (1974 reprinted in 1978, 1980, 1985); *Langakali* (Mana Publications, Suva, 1981, 1982, 1983, 1991); *Inselfeuer* (Reihe Literatur des Pazifik, Nuremburg, 1986); *Hingano* (Mana Publications, Suva, 1987); *Kakala* (Mana Publications, Suva, 1993).

27 *Tai, Heart of a Tree* (New Women's Press, Auckland, 1988), back cover.

28 *Solaua, a Secret Embryo* (Mana Publications, Suva, 1979); *Paa Alimago on Wet Days* (1979); *Alaoa, Above the Gully of Your Childhood* (Western Samoa Historical and Cultural Trust, Apia, Western Samoa, 1986). A total collection is found in Von Reiche's 1988 publication. There is also a collection of short stories *Maunu Mai Loimata o 'Apa'ula* (I.P.S., Western Samoa Extension Centre of University of the South Pacific Suva, Fiji; Iunivesite Aoao o Samoa, Apia, Western Samoa, 1987).

29 *Black Stone* (Mana Publications, Suva, 1983); *Colonised People* (Black Stone Publications, Port Vila, 1980); *Black Stone II* (Black Stone Publications and Vanuatu University of the South Pacific Extension Centre, Vanuatu, 1989). Molisa has also published numerous articles and booklets on politics, women, and art.

30 In 1905, Tonga was supervised by a British Consul who had virtual veto rights over pivotal government decisions. However, Tonga largely maintained its centralised power base because of the absolute prohibition on any private ownership of land (Campbell, pp. 199, 177).

31 'I Tremble' in Thaman, *You, The Choice of My Parents*, p. 2.

32 Thaman, *Langakali*, p. 2.

33 Germany annexed Western Samoa in 1899, while the United States annexed Eastern Samoa, still known as American Samoa today (Campbell, pp. 136-49).

34 After World War I, the establishment of the Permanent Mandates Commission of the new League of Nations saw the German colony of Samoa placed under a New Zealand protectorate.

35 'Solaua, a secret embryo', in Von Reiche, *Solaua, A Secret Embryo*, p. 2.

36 Momoe Malietoa married into the Von Reiche family who have a firmly established German mercantile presence in Samoa.

37 The rubber tree (*Hevea Brasiliensis* was the most popular strain) was introduced to Western Samoa by planters some time during 1893. It started producing in 1906 with the intervention of the German colonial government but never superceded the planting or exporting of cacao or coconuts.

38 'Above the Gully of Your Childhood,' in Von Reiche, *Alaoa, Above the Gully of Your Childhood* .

39 Usually a brown woman suffers over the infidelities of her *palagi* (white), often German, husband.

40 The first of its kind in the world.

41 This term often facetiously replaced the official terminology.

42 Molisa, *Black Stone II*, p. 10.

43 Ibid, p. 9.

44 Both her collections are published under 'Sipolo', the last name from her first marriage.

45 Sipolo, 1981, p. 21.

46 bell hooks, *Black Looks: Race and Representation* (South End Press, Boston, 1992), p. 3.

47 Originally a non-Pacific delineation, these regional distinctions are problematic and have often served to divide the Pacific, despite many cultural similarities in disparate regions.

48 Campbell, p. 218.

49 Trask argues that indigenous men were especially vulnerable to being corrupted by patriarchal colonialism since only men's authority was recognised and preyed upon. See Haunani-Kay Trask *From A Native Daughter: Colonialism and Sovereignty in Hawai'i* (Common Courage Press, Monroe, Maine, 1993).

50 Thaman, *You, The Choice of My Parents*, p. 5.

51 See Barbara Smith, *Home Girls: A Black Feminist Anthology* (Kitchen Table and Women of Color Press, New York, 1983); Susheila Nasta (ed.), *Motherlands: Black Women's Writing from Africa, the Caribbean, and South East Asia* (Rutgers University Press, New Brunswick, N.J., 1992); Robin Morgan (ed.), *Sisterhood is Global: The International Women's Movement Anthology* (Anchor Books, Doubleday, Garden City, New York, 1984).

52 Molara Ogundipe-Leslie, 'Nigeria: Not Spinning on the Axis of Maleness', in Morgan, pp. 498-504, 499.

53 Michelle Vizzard, '"Of Mimicry and Woman": Hysteria and Anticolonial Feminism in Tsitsi Dangarembga's *Nervous Conditions*', *Span*, 36:1 (1993), pp. 202-10.

54 Ogundipe-Leslie in Morgan, p. 500.

55 'In Algeria, many of us, including myself, kept silent for ten years after Independence, not to give fuel to the enemies of the glorious Algerian revolution ... I will certainly admit that Western right-wing forces may and will use our protests, especially if they remain isolated. But it is as true to say that our own rightist forces exploit our silence.' Marie-Aimée Hèlie-Lucas, 'Bound and Gagged by the Family Code', Miranda Davies (ed.), *Third World – Second Sex: Women's Struggles and National Liberation* (Zed Books, London, 1987), pp. 2, 14. See also Morgan, p. 334.

56 Palestinian Fawzia Fawzia in Morgan, p. 540.

57 Fawzia points out that no 'target date' has yet been set to deal with the 'woman question', ibid., p. 541.

58 Fatma Oussedik from Algeria speaks of 'the daughters of those women who waged a liberation war and whose only liberation was to return to their kitchens ...' Getting to the heart of the matter Oussedik asserts the core of the struggle she is involved with for women's liberation: '*It's about women who, while challenging the oppression under which they live, necessarily challenge all forms of oppression.*' (Morgan, p. 48). In Vanuatu, many of the grassroots movements for independence were led and supported by women. However, as has been the experience of women the world over, little recognition was given to women when forming the new Nation. As was the case in Vanuatu, seven years after Independence, prominent female leaders in the nationalist movement as well in the community were questioning the validity of Independence for them. See Grace Molisa (ed.), 'Nasonol Festivol Blong Ol Woman' *Who Will Carry The Bag?* (Port Vila, n.d.).

59 La Silencida, Cuban revolutionary, in Morgan, p. 176.

60 See also Atu Emberson-Bain (ed.), *Malignant Growth or Sustainable Development? Perspectives of Pacific Island Women* (Marama Publications, Suva, Fiji, 1994).

61 Two United States presidents have publicly acknowledged and apologised for the illegal American overthrow of the Hawaiian Government: President Cleveland soon after the actual event, and in 1995 President Clinton. No formal action was taken then to right the wrongs. None has been taken now.

62 Hawai'i part 6, 'E Pele e, fire-eater from Kahiki', Trask, p. 36.

63 This is an ever-pressing problem in Hawai'i and several Hawaiians have used the analogy to refer to the colonial situation.

64 See in this collection her poems 'Marriage', 'Pregnant Blues', 'Ladies of Precedence', 'Status Costs' which also deliver strong 'feminist' statements that critique women's subordination via custom and societal expectations, and analyse strong female leadership.

65 Grace Mera Molisa, *Woman Ikat Raet Long Human Raet O No?: Convention on the Elimination of All Forms of Discrimination Against Women* (Australian High Commission, Port Vila, Sun Productions, Port Vila, Vanuatu, n.d.).

66 See Molisa (1989), 'Fridom', p. 35, 'Lost Horizon', p. 17.

67 Molisa uses this stylistic device in other poems in her 1987 collection.

68 This publication was funded by the Australian High Commission, Port Vila (Sun Productions, Port Vila).

69 Black is a foundational colour on the National flag symbolising Melanesian people. Unity is one of the values espoused in the national slogan which asserts 'Unity, Peace, Prosperity', Joel Bonnemaison, *Vanuatu* (Les Editions Du Pacifique, Singapore, 1986), p. 19.

70 In a booklet Grace Mera Molisa wrote and published called *Indigenous Arts Communications Networking* (Blackstone, Port Vanuatu, 1994), a result of her experience of participating in the Indigenous Artists' Conference 'Beyond Survival' (Ottawa, Canada, 1993), she emphasises that the role and integrity of the artist is dependent upon 'Honesty and Sincerity' and a total commitment to truth as artists are 'people skilled in expressing the feelings and visions of their people ... [artists] play an essential role in establishing, recording, documenting and preserving the Cultural Identity of their people, their experiences, feelings and situations of their time'(ibid., p. 29).

71 Susanna Ounei-Small,'Decolonising Feminism', *Tok Blong Pasifik*, 49:2 (1995), p. 20.